Succeeding as a Deputy Head

OTHER TITLES IN THE *SUCCEEDING AS...* SERIES:

Succeeding as a Head of Year by Jon Tait

Succeeding as an English Teacher by Abigail Mann

Succeeding as a Maths Teacher by Caroline Kennedy, Amie Meek, Emma Weston and Gemma Sherwood

Succeeding as a History Teacher by Emily Folorunsho and Laura Gladwin

Succeeding as an MFL Teacher by Sylvia Bastow and Jennifer Wozniak-Rush

Succeeding as an RE Teacher Edited by Andy Lewis

Succeeding as a Deputy Head

**ADAM KOHLBECK
& CHRIS PASSEY**

BLOOMSBURY EDUCATION
LONDON OXFORD NEW YORK NEW DELHI SYDNEY

BLOOMSBURY EDUCATION
Bloomsbury Publishing Plc
50 Bedford Square, London WC1B 3DP, UK
Bloomsbury Publishing Ireland Limited
29 Earlsfort Terrace, Dublin 2, D02 AY28, Ireland

BLOOMSBURY, BLOOMSBURY EDUCATION and the
Diana logo are trademarks of Bloomsbury Publishing Plc

First published in Great Britain 2026 by Bloomsbury Publishing Plc
This edition published in Great Britain 2026 by Bloomsbury Publishing Plc

Text copyright © Chris Passey and Adam Kohlbeck, 2026

Chris Passey and Adam Kohlbeck have asserted their rights under the
Copyright, Designs and Patents Act, 1988, to be identified as Authors of
this work.

All rights reserved. No part of this publication may be: i) reproduced or
transmitted in any form, electronic or mechanical, including photocopying,
recording or by means of any information storage or retrieval system
without prior permission in writing from the publishers; or ii) used
or reproduced in any way for the training, development or operation
of artificial intelligence (AI) technologies, including generative AI
technologies. The rights holders expressly reserve this publication from
the text and data mining exception as per Article 4(3) of the Digital Single
Market Directive (EU) 2019/790

A catalogue record for this book is available from the British Library

ISBN: PB: 978-1-80199-619-8; ePub: 978-1-80199-621-1

2 4 6 8 10 9 7 5 3 1 (paperback)

Cover design by James Fraser
Typeset by Lumina Datamatics

Printed and bound in Great Britain by TJ Books, Padstow, Cornwall

To find out more about our authors and books visit www.bloomsbury.com
and sign up for our newsletters
For product safety related questions contact productsafety@bloomsbury.com

Dedications

Adam

For my wife, Lea, in thanks for her unwavering patience, love and support.

For my parents for the encouragement they have always shown and for my son, Joshua, my purpose and inspiration.

Chris

For Attiye, my amazing wife who supports me in all of my many, many plots and plans:
Nakupenda sana mpenzi wangu.
For Nigel, Ryan and Lucy, and for Juno and Delilah: reading is the gift that keeps on giving and this is the book I promised to write for you.

Contents

Acknowledgements ix
Foreword xi

Introduction 1

PART 1: Foundations of Leadership

1 Headteacher alignment 11
2 Establishing and managing relationships 35
3 Building trust and setting standards 57
4 Leading whole school areas 79

PART 2: Cultivating personal and professional growth

5 Developing support staff 115
6 Developing teachers 137
7 Developing leaders 169
8 Developing yourself 191
9 Conclusion: bridging the gap 213

Your first 90 days as Deputy Headteacher 218
A note from the authors 225
References 229
Index 237

Acknowledgements

We would like to express our heartfelt gratitude to the extraordinary individuals who have shared their professional perspectives on how to succeed as a Deputy Head. Their words of wisdom have allowed our small contribution to the conversation remain relevant and grounded: Sally Alexander MBE, Sam Gibbs, Andrew Percival, Gwyn Ap Harri, Hannah Abbiss, Josh Goodrich, Guy Shears, Richard Skilbeck, Attiye Passey, Lekha Sharma, Shaun Passey, Anna Woodcock, Clare Hoods-Truman, Swabra Lloyd, Keith Slade and Stuart Milne.

Beyond the professional perspectives within this book, we also wish to acknowledge the contributions, advice and guidance given to us over the past year as this book took shape. This book is richer and more informative thanks to their insights and experience. Leadership should never be embarked upon alone and we owe a great debt to these extraordinary people: Professor Paul Miller, Dr Philip Purvis, Sarah Cottinghatt, Joanna Tompkins, Peter Monk, Professor Dr. Haili Hughes, Professor Nigel Pattinson, Alex Hawthorn, Siobhan King, Caroline Sherwood, Yamina Bibi, Shane Leaning and Professer Sam Twiselton OBE.

The authors

Adam Kohlbeck

MA PGDip BA (Hons) CMgr FCMI FCCT
Adam Kohlbeck is a Deputy Headteacher, working in South-East London. He is also the co-founder of the EduPulse think tank

and has 16 years of teaching experience, the last six of which have been spent as a Senior leader. He has published work in both the Chartered College of Teaching and Primary First journals and is a Fellow of the College, with whom he also holds Chartered status. Adam holds a master's degree in Educational Leadership and is currently studying for a professional doctorate in Education. He sits on an industry advisory board for the National Institute of Teaching and Education and has supported numerous schools across London with their development priorities in a consultancy capacity. He is a regular speaker, podcaster and writer, with a particular interest and expertise in professional development (PD) and leadership.

Chris Passey

MA PGDip CMgr FCMI FIoL FCCT FRSA
Chris Passey is Headteacher at Kimichi School, a small music specialist school in the West Midlands where he also serves as a Chair of Governors at Waseley Hills Secondary School. A proud Fellow of the Chartered College of Teaching, Chris holds a master's degree in Educational Leadership from Coventry University and is also a Fellow of the Chartered Management Institute, the Institute of Leadership and the Royal Society of Arts. With a passion for SEND advocacy and context dependent leadership, Chris trains independent school SENDCos for the Independent Schools Association and sits on the industry advisory board for the National Institute of Teaching and Education, as well as being a non-executive director of the Association of Education Advisors. Chris is a published children's author and channels his passion for writing and teaching into co-leading English at his school as well as professional development and teaching and learning, all whilst sitting in his office alongside his Dachshund, Pablo.

Foreword

Prof Sam Twiselton, OBE – Emeritus Professor

Who are the change agents in schools? The catalysts who not only ignite the spark but also develop and sustain the momentum to make that change long term and embedded? In my experience the answer is very often the Deputy Head – the unsung doers who make things happen. In my many engagements with schools over the years I have observed the unique challenges and opportunities that accompany this role. Deputies must constantly face both ways – having a close and engaged relationship with strategic priorities while working with and supporting those immersed in the day-to-day realities of the chalkface.

Adam and Chris not only recognise and celebrate this but they give reflective insights into why and how the role is so important to the effective running of schools. They recognise the critical role that relationships – the life blood of a successful learning community – play in being a successful deputy. Leading, managing and supporting productive relationships is central to effective leadership and the deputy is right at the heart of this. Deputies need to have their fingers on the pulse of the whole school community, and this can only happen if there is a culture of open communication, trust and respect fostered through relationships.

These aspects of leadership are examined through the superbly useful approaches carried consistently throughout the book. So many authors who write about leadership raise important themes at an abstract level but fail to sufficiently guide readers into the practicalities that mean they can action anything. Adam and Chris include relatable case studies relayed with humanity and humour and other examples that avoid this trap. Tools and activities are included to bridge the gap between the issues discussed and what they mean for the reader's own context. The approach is systematically evidence based, with a range of relevant studies. The findings and implications of these are presented in an accessible and implementable way. The combination of evidence, practice and personal reflection is designed to build confidence and resilience, alongside enthusiasm and positivity.

The final brilliant aspect of this book that excited me in its connection to my own research is the importance of professional identity and growth. This is threaded throughout in relation to the role of deputies in supporting growth in others but also (importantly) recognises this as key element for the role holders themselves. Finding, revisiting and enacting our own personal 'why' is an important part of being a fulfilled educator that is often dominant and conscious as someone chooses to enter the profession but can easily be lost or become invisible in the everyday business of the school and classroom. Nurturing and prioritising our moral compass and the principles for action that arise from this is so important and it is great that this is given prominence.

Enjoy your journey through this great book – whether it is linear or of the dip in and out variety – it will not only feed your enthusiasm but give you great ideas to implement in your own context.

Introduction

The curious position of balance

Succeeding as a Deputy Headteacher is largely dependent on successfully navigating the many challenges that come with the role. In fact, the requirements of the role make it perhaps the most demanding in a school. How do you balance strategic thinking with the vast array of operational issues that keep a school running? Furthermore, how does a Deputy Head accomplish this when they are not the ultimate decision maker or work distributor? The need to implement systems – some of which you may have had limited design input – while also understanding the individual contexts of every member of the school community is another frequent challenge for the Deputy Head.

In this role, you must remain optimistically ambitious whilst also being brutally realistic; otherwise, generating belief in your direction, and in your leadership is an uphill struggle. You must instil faith in your followers with certainty while also being willing to embrace vulnerability and fallibility. The paradoxical roles of judgement and development often also fall at the door of the Deputy Head. This can lead to a state of such urgency that paralysis of action results, when in fact thinking slow and acting fast (Kahneman, 2012) is the desirable mindset.

We are now co-authors, and we first met on our master's degree in educational leadership. We were there to learn and, we thought, to apply our learning directly into our own contexts. However, while our schools have benefitted from what we learned in both practical and theoretical contexts, the most valuable thing we took from the course was the way we were able to reconceptualise the notion of successful leadership. This is what we want to share with you, our readers. We don't aim to give you 'the answers'. Instead, we hope that our perspective, our insight and our experience will give you the space and inspiration to examine your own leadership against your context and ultimately, succeed – whatever that means for you.

Succeeding as a Deputy Headteacher is a multifaceted and context driven endeavour. In a modern education system that offers increasingly diverse opportunities for career development, success in a leadership role is now about much more than successfully applying for headship. The role of Headteacher – often equally paradoxical – is now so varied from one context to another that a well-rounded leadership grounding is essential before taking that step.

The successful Deputy Headteacher will master relationships and all the complex and nuanced detail that this entails. Trust, motivation, purpose, meaning, care and respect are all intangible relational aspects that a school leader must become adept at balancing. However, a Deputy Head occupies that position of having – often literally – one foot in the classroom and one foot out. They exist without the final veto that sits with the Headteacher but also without the respectful dissent that is afforded to a class teacher among a close group of trusted colleagues. Achieving and sustaining effective relationships to help drive improvement is a significant challenge. Driving this challenge is the presence of obstacles or pressures that pop up at almost every turn.

How does a successful Deputy Headteacher maintain trust among their colleagues when they are simultaneously responsible for:

- Developing confident members of staff, and
- Contributing to evaluative processes that monitor school improvement (which inevitably involve criticism and judgement)?

This book aims to help Deputy Headteachers navigate these responsibilities and other key challenges including how to develop leaders, how to work with your Headteacher and how to lead on multiple areas in your school.

How to read this book

You can read *Succeeding as a Deputy Head* from cover to cover or use it as a reference guide for dipping in and out of, as and when challenges arise. Each chapter provides digestible advice from notable and influential voices in education.

Foundations of leadership

This section of the book focuses on how the successful Deputy Headteacher needs to prioritise relationships and trust by examining, establishing and managing relationships, building trust, setting standards and aligning with the Headteacher.

Cultivating personal and professional growth

One of the biggest roles of any Deputy Head is the myriad ways in which we can influence the development, both professional and personal, of support staff, teachers, potential leaders and ultimately, ourselves. We examine case studies and practical examples of school leaders who have achieved success in developing the skillsets of people within their organisations and, as a result, the organisations themselves.

We are *not* suggesting that this is the definitive or ultimate way to be or succeed as a Deputy Head. However, for us, this book is an homage to our thinking, research and experience working in schools about what it takes to become successful in educational leadership. It's not *the* only way, but we do hope you'll find it useful.

Before you dive in, it is worth highlighting the generous expertise of our contributors, who enrich each chapter. From across the sector, they bring a wealth of experience, a wide range of viewpoints, decency, humility and authenticity to each of their contributions. As you take your first steps into this book, and perhaps, into Deputy Headship, we offer the first of many guiding voices who share their views on what makes a successful Deputy Headteacher. Sally Alexander MBE is the Founder and Executive Headteacher of Kimichi Schools and Stuart Milne is Deputy Head of Oxted School, Surrey. They both offer a unique view on what makes a successful Deputy Head.

We hope that this book will encourage you to embrace the complexities and the challenges of the role. The paradoxes and obstacles that exist in the Deputy Headteacher's world demand a lot. You will make mistakes, as we all do, but above all, those same challenges offer you the opportunity to understand the role in its full glory. Anticipating the trickier moments and using this book as a tool to help you find the appropriate strategies to bridge the gap will be fulfilling and purposeful work. With that, we truly hope that this book will help you to embrace the paradox and succeed as a Deputy Headteacher.

PROFESSIONAL PERSPECTIVE

By Stuart Milne – Deputy Head of Oxted School, Surrey

My first professional role was not as a teacher but in sales for a large Transnational Corporation (TNC), operating in the fast-moving consumer goods sector. The one thing I have always remembered from this time is that 'we were selling ideas, not products'. That has remained with me throughout my teaching career. As leaders, we must sell the idea, and from that position, you can capture hearts and minds. From this place you will have mobilised a team that has the same focus and reason for working hard.

There are so many people (colleagues, students and people at home) whom I have been fortunate to work with who have helped me to grow as a person and as a leader. It is not one thing that will help you to become a great Deputy Headteacher but some of the ideas that I have found are below.

The magic happens when:

- you have arrived at what is important to you and that you live by these values
- you see the person, you are interested in them, you take time to know them
- you empower those you work with by creating opportunities that will help them to realise the great things that they can achieve
- people know what you are going to say before you say it
- you understand the importance of positive relationships with students, staff and people at home
- you can 'be calm, be clear, be kind'.

PROFESSIONAL PERSPECTIVE

by Sally Alexander MBE, founder and executive Headteacher of Kimichi Schools

For the first couple of years of my headship at school, I didn't have the luxury of a Deputy Head. In fact, I didn't have the luxury of another teacher at all. This is all fine when you have a handful of pupils, but as my school grew it was inevitable that more staff would be needed.

I have been incredibly fortunate to have a staff team that has organically evolved and strengthened over the past ten years. Every day has been a learning experience for all of us, and we have embraced those opportunities for growth together. This is especially true of my Deputy Headteacher, who initially joined as a Primary teacher and, through dedication to the school and its ethos, as well as hard work, has become one of the foundational pillars of the school. His journey reflects not only his commitment but also his exceptional achievements, earning a remarkable array of qualifications and school-based acronyms that reflect his unwavering commitment to excellence.

Those learning experiences have included:

- **Listening:** it's essential to listen to what you're being asked or told. It's just as important to listen for what's not being said in the moment.
- **Approachability:** hiding behind the barricade of your 'lofty' position endears you to no one and is not conducive to building any form of cohesive staff relationship.
- **Communication:** it's such an obvious point to make, and yet it needs to be reiterated every day. Communication between staff, pupils and parents is never ending, and

that's how it should be. School works best when home, school and pupil all communicate.
- **Mind reading:** you must be well-aligned with the ethos of the Deputy Headteacher that when faced with difficult decisions, you know what they would be thinking and, most of the time, you know what they would decide. That doesn't mean you must always do the same thing but if you do make a different decision from the one you know they would have made, you are at least ready to explain your decision in the context of their expectations.
- **Calm:** the ability to stay calm when the world around you is heading towards chaos. Amidst the turmoil, it's our job to protect our pupils and ensure that any extra noise is never allowed to drown out that fundamental fact.
- **Bouncing:** to have a Deputy Head in sync with you, your ideas, your school ethos and your drive and ambition is worth its weight in gold. Part of that is the ability to bounce ideas off each other, both positive and negative; awkward conversations are awkward for a reason, but important nonetheless.

Finally, remaining true to the *soul* of your school. *Ethos* is simply not strong enough a word here. If you live and breathe your school, and allow your staff to do the same, it's a journey you're on together, and that can only be for the benefit of everyone involved.

PART 1

Foundations of leadership

1

Headteacher alignment

Being a Deputy Head is about your relationship with the Headteacher and how this very specific dynamic can weather the myriad storms that will batter and bruise the shoreline, or cliff edge, of your working and personal relationship.

When planning this chapter, we decided that 'alignment' was the term that captured all of the nuances that come with a Deputy-Headteacher relationship where you:

- Fully support and agree in all areas.
- Support but sometimes disagree on points of policy or culture.
- Get on socially but fundamentally disagree with their way of working.

...and so many more. We felt 'aligning' was the best verb we could use to describe a relationship where mutual acceptance of fundamental differences allows you both to get on with the day-to-day business of running a school. For us, aligning with your Headteacher speaks to a willingness to compromise, adaptable leadership styles and your ability to reserve your thoughts and feelings for the good of the school.

What's in a title?

The advent of Multi-Academy Trusts (MATs) brought about a fundamental change in leadership structures throughout the UK education system. Governing bodies that sit above a single school can now be consolidated into a single Local Governing Body (LGB) that strategically oversees the management and performance of multiple schools. Posts such as Executive, Associate and Assistant Headteacher were created above a traditional Headteacher who may have seen their title change to Head of School. MATs, local authority maintained schools and independent settings each have their own unique set of hierarchical rules and norms, with the size of the setting determining the number of various subsets of Headteachers. The diagram below attempts to outline a generic hierarchy of responsibility within schools, with dotted boxes denoting roles that other schools may have as a result of their unique structures.

A study looking at the changing role of the Headteacher, conducted by Lewis et. al (2023), found that the roles of Headteachers and Heads of Schools in MATs were 'operating in roles with considerable contradictions' (p.23). Their responsibility for teaching and learning was at odds with their power over strategic and operational decisions relating to HR, IT and finance. For example, in some larger MATs, Headteachers are highly accountable for teaching outcomes yet have comparatively little control over centralised approaches to teaching. It's also worth noting that those in the study struggled with the contradiction between the needs of the trust as a whole and the context specific issues of individual schools. Comparisons can be drawn, in other structures, between the goals of the Headteacher, who has overall control of the school's culture and vision, and the Deputy, who may be more concerned with the inner workings of the school itself.

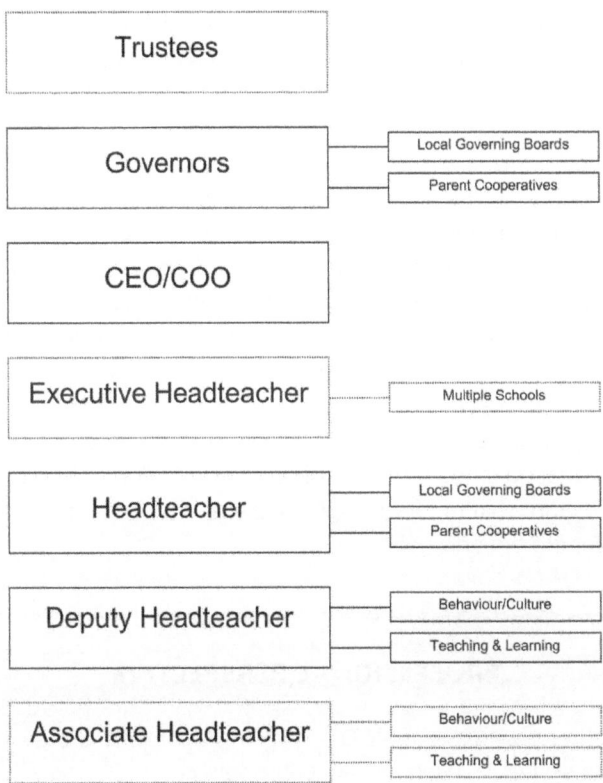

FIGURE 1: *Generic hierarchy of varying school leadership models*

Despite a title change, it remains that the Head ('teacher' or 'of school') retains the power to suspend, exclude and otherwise dictate the day-to-day running of the school. As a Deputy, it is your official responsibility to speak for or act on behalf of the Headteacher when they are not present or are unable to fulfil their duties. Unlike an Assistant or Associate, you possess the ability to take on the actionable and executive 'powers' of the Headteacher when it comes to suspension or exclusion.

So, what's in a title? For Deputy Headteachers, it can carry significant meaning and it shouldn't ever be taken for granted. As we'll discuss in Chapter 7, certain personalities and leadership styles will not be suited to this responsibility. Authoritative and ambitious leaders may struggle with the slight subservience that occurs in their own minds; we have heard one Deputy compare their job to being an heir apparent 'waiting for the monarch to die' before being crowned. There's no doubt that, no matter how efficient or promising the candidate, this type of thinking is bound to end in disaster. We acknowledge that not all Deputy Heads wish to pursue the role of Headteacher, as outlined in Chapter 9.

Gwyn Ap Harri is the CEO of the XP Trust, and we asked him what he thought Headteachers should look for in a Deputy Head, and what red flags might be present when ambition and power are the only goals.

PROFESSIONAL PERSPECTIVE

By Gwyn Ap Harri – CEO of XP Trust, comprising three secondary schools and five primary schools in Doncaster. XP Trust is a Multi-Academy Trust that delivers the curriculum through cross-curricular expeditions linked to real world experiences.

Let's assume you're in the position where you feel you have found a Deputy Head who has the energy, capability and drive to take up your mantle. You are most likely friends, confidants and have a few miles of shared experience.

You've 'done' your job, you lack energy for it, and it deserves the rush of new blood. They'll bring their own style and things will inevitably change, but the essence of what you have built, the culture you have nurtured, is strong and this is what will ensure the continuing success of the organisation. Right? Any doubts are wiped away with thoughts of, 'They're young, they'll learn, they'll get it. They'll probably do a better job than me!'

You are in a vulnerable position. You hold the power to make either a great decision or one of the worst decisions of your life, which will affect other lives too. You are the metaphorical frog in a pan of warm water. The saying goes that to boil a frog, you can't drop it in a pan of boiling water; it will just jump out to safety. No, to boil a frog, you have to place it in a pan of lukewarm water and slowly raise the temperature so it doesn't notice until it's too late.

Hope on max, looking to the future elsewhere, trusted sidekick – the water's feeling lovely and warm! I would say that one of my strengths is to see and accept 'reality' rather than 'perception' and even I found myself in this position. How do you spot this, and how do you ensure you won't be in the same position again?

The words 'hope' and 'trust' need examining here. Hope is the feeling that someone will do the right thing in the future, even when you have doubts. Trust is the same, but without the doubts. Hope is what a person driven by ego and fear will trade on. They will build this up in you. Hope is empty and you cannot see it. 'Don't worry, I've got it...' If you have 'hope', you have nothing. The dangerous deputy will give you hope readily.

Trust is often misunderstood. Most people think that you have to show your trust in someone by allowing them to take something on without supervision. If you ask someone to show you their work and they respond with, 'Don't you trust me?' – that's a red flag. Real 'trust' is transactional: 'I am giving you my trust to do something important for me. In return you will show me your work, unfinished and open to critique so we can make high quality decisions and produce high quality work together as a team. Be proud of your work and share it often, letting me know your progress and hurdles.' Real trust is built through purposeful collaboration, strong relationships and shared challenges.

If someone doesn't share what they are doing, how it is going, what successes they have had and issues they are facing, don't trust them. But most importantly – you must 'see' their work, not just 'hear' about it. Building an organisation with a culture of making work public is to build an organisation based on reality and not perception. When you 'see' their work, and judge its quality, do not have hope. Be kind, specific and helpful. Show compassionate candour, not ruinous empathy.

This is what you should look for in a deputy: high quality decision making through problem solving and empowerment, by looking at their work, not just hearing about it.

The other thing you should look out for is 'separation'.

As empowering leaders, we must be acutely vigilant for signs of disconnection within our team, especially when it's done deliberately to gain power. The divide-and-conquer strategy is often driven by ego and fear and tends to undermine trust and collaboration.

In my situation, this tactic became so absurdly obvious. When I finally stopped taking the word of this person and spoke directly with the people they were controlling and manipulating through separation (including me), their house of cards literally crumbled overnight. When we started putting everyone back together, we realised the reality of the situation and the many untruths and deception unravelled.

> We now have a mantra: 'Get the right people in the room together!' – facilitating high-quality communication to form a shared conceptual understanding and commit to the consensus.
>
> The next CEO of XP Trust will work alongside me, then just in front of me, then from afar but never out of sight. They will embrace criticism, openness and transparency. They will produce high-quality work with others, building teams themselves, celebrating and sharing their work publicly and together. They will solve problems by empowering their team.
>
> I will not hope they do a good job when I step aside. I will have no doubt, because they will show others that they can do it.

Gwyn's insight is honest, raw and thought-provoking and it demonstrates the fragility of leadership at all levels.

PERSONAL REFLECTION

Did anything Gwyn say resonate with you? What elements of Gwyn's perspective apply to your setting or personal story and can you take any lessons from them?

_____
_____
_____
_____
_____

For us, the striking reality is that trust and hope are linked in a transactional way:

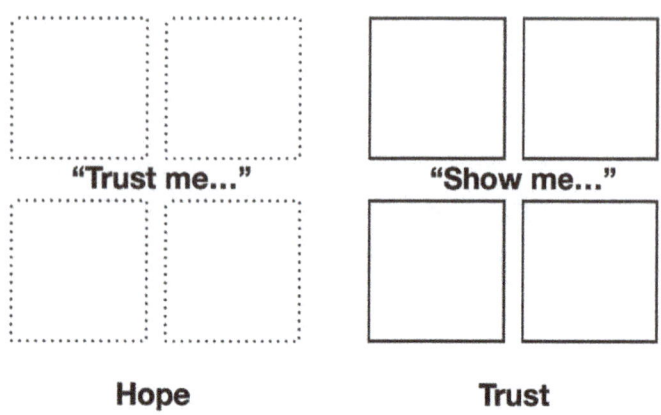

FIGURE 2: *Model of hope versus trust, based on Gwyn Ap Harri's perspective*

Figure 2 demonstrates that a position of 'trust me' is a weaker position whereby your leaders are hoping you have done the work or job required. In contrast, a request for proof should be viewed as a solid confirmation of trust; a transactional process that benefits everyone. If your Headteacher or leader isn't asking for proof of your work but rather 'trusting' you to do your job, they are trading in hope and opening themselves up to harm should you not complete the job. For Deputy Heads, this could jeopardise organisational security or safeguarding and welfare. Instead, you can anticipate this potential blind spot by producing and insisting on presenting your work as a display of transactional trust; doing so will likely cement your reliability and conscientious working habits with your Head. If your Head is asking for proof of your work, see it as an opportunity to reward their trust in you and complete the transaction with pride.

Understanding Headteacher leadership

Male and Wright (2015) conducted a study of an Headteacher internship that involved placing Deputy Heads in the Head role for a period of four weeks to assess the leadership implications of such a move. The results were surprising in that the intern took on their new role with aplomb, despite fundamentally believing the role was not for them. In contrast, the Headteacher, who switched to Deputy, struggled to relinquish control with a reluctance that nearly led to the end of the internship and the study as a whole. The study concluded that, whilst the Head struggled, there were important learning moments for the future of the school's SLT model moving forward. The intern enjoyed the additional responsibility and would consider a promotion should one become available.

There is a moment when one crosses the threshold between Deputy and Headteacher and it is increasingly important that prospective Deputy Heads know what lies beyond that line and whether or not they are suitably equipped for the role (see Chapter 8). Crucially, however, this threshold works for the Head who struggled to step back and for whom alignment had previously meant clearly defined barriers of power. We would boldly suggest that whilst obvious and accepted roles and divestments of power are needed, true alignment manifests when the Deputy and Headteacher work as a partnership.

We believe that successful alignment comes from addressing the following areas: noting the ideal circumstances for success, recognising signs that may indicate a challenge or difficult conversation is needed and conducting those conversations effectively.

Supportive alignment

As the second-in-command, the Deputy Headteacher is expected to align with the Headteacher's vision, goals and decisions regarding all aspects of school life. This alignment is crucial for maintaining consistency, unity and effective leadership within the school. Whilst this may seem obvious, partnership is far more important than restrictive attitudes on roles and powers. Headteachers keenly feel isolation in their roles (Mercer, 1996) and this could lead to lower engagement with their leadership teams through weakened group dynamics and, perhaps, a decrease in their usual leadership style (Lam and Lau, 2012).

Tips for success

- Honest and open conversations about culture, beliefs and ethics around education. This should be an ongoing conversation between the two of you and should have been addressed during the interview stage.

- Share your experiences in other settings and what made you feel comfortable and appreciated, or not, from other leadership models. Ensure this is done without overusing the phrase 'in my previous school'. Your context is important but your current school requires a clean slate and fresh approach.

- Ensure that, despite any differences, you can come to a shared understanding (see page 25).

Red flags

- Withdrawal of the Head from whole-school activities including assemblies, open events and staff meetings.
- Arguments or disagreements that go beyond simple principles but that speak to a more fundamental disagreement; think of a couple in a relationship that suddenly discovers the other doesn't want children. Sometimes, fundamental differences are beyond repair and require a different mindset to continue running the school capturing everyone's best interests.

Critical engagement

Even if you find yourself in perfect alignment with your Head, you have a responsibility to engage critically with the Headteacher's ideas and decisions. This needs to be done in a positive way where you provide constructive feedback, offer alternative perspectives and challenge assumptions when necessary.

Tips for success

- Think holistically about a problem and make the effort to become a solution-led leader. Consider how all the elements of a problem interact with each other rather than looking at each one in isolation.
- Your ability to empathise with, or appreciate, and understand the viewpoint of your Headteacher is essential.

Red flags

- A 'my way or the highway' attitude without cause or reason is a sign of relationship breakdown. There are times when the senior leadership needs to employ a less than desirable change 'to' rather than 'with' approach
- A Headteacher who is gatekeeping their thought processes and motives rather than your alignment with them, even for the sake of stability, is impossible.

Advocating for staff

You may find yourself playing devil's advocate so that staff push back is mitigated before it arises. Sometimes this insight will have come from direct conversations with staff; this type of advocacy may sometimes involve challenging or translating decisions made by the Headteacher if they are perceived to be detrimental to the staff or the overall functioning of the school.

Tips for success

- Share your concerns or wider staff concerns promptly. Communicate them clearly and without bias to the Headteacher.
- Be transparent and honest, always.

Red flags

- Be wary of appearing too partisan, which can sometimes result in an 'us vs them' situation.

Maybe more than most, this is a true test of your leadership style and how others receive it. You are there to take in one point of view and deliver it with compassion and empathy to other key decision makers.

- Your Headteacher should have empathy for your role and the awkward position you can find yourself in at times. Moments where you doubt this, from either side, should be approached with caution. Honest and authentic conversations with your Headteacher will more likely lead to honest and authentic results, even if you may disagree.

Maintaining trust

Building and maintaining trust between the Deputy Headteacher and the Headteacher is essential. It fosters open and honest communication, even in the face of disagreements. Trust also enables the Deputy Headteacher to challenge decisions without undermining the authority or leadership of the Headteacher.

Tips for success

- Lead authentically to build trust with your Headteacher, particularly during instances of disagreement (see Chapter 4).
- Maintain trust by explicitly agreeing that what is discussed will not leave the room, accompanied by obvious public support of one another.

Red flags

- As Gwyn ap Hari said earlier, trust is misunderstood. Leaders who unquestioningly trust without scrutiny are trading in hope alone. Look out for leaders who are happy for you to 'get on with it' without checking your work. This can sometimes hinder opportunities for collaborative growth for both parties.

Promoting collaboration

Finding opportunities for collaboration between the Deputy Headteacher and the Headteacher fosters a culture of teamwork and shared responsibility. Collaboration allows for different perspectives to be considered, resulting in more informed and robust decision making processes.

Tips for success

- Find times to show the school that you're in lockstep with one another; assemblies and sectional school gatherings (optimistic, we know!) provide the perfect opportunity to demonstrate your shared concept of culture and message.

Red flags

- As Gwyn ap Harri alluded to earlier, a shared conceptual understanding is crucial (see page 14).
- Be alert to moments where your Headteacher announces policy areas or whole-school notices over

which you would usually have responsibility. This may well be an oversight. You should feel comfortable enough to begin a calm, professional conversation about it.

> **CONVERSATION STARTERS**
>
> - I feel like X is an accurate view of what is happening at the moment. I'd like to hear your thoughts in response to that…
> - Can we run through the thought process behind X so that I have full understanding, in case I am asked?
> - Could we clarify what your expectations are of me within the context of X?
> - Is it possible to make sure that we are fully aligned on X because I think my current understanding is not wholly accurate?

Establishing ethos and culture – what is shared understanding?

Think of a time when you've engaged in a mutual agreement with someone: *if you get this drink, I'll get the next one; I'll do your printing when you're off sick and you'll do the same for me. You do the cooking and I'll do the washing up.* These are all examples of an unspoken agreement.

We all have friends for whom we abandoned the 'lifts given vs pints bought' tally many years ago and we continue to joke about one day balancing it out despite the gulf of time. It's funny and representative of many years of friendship which is rarely replicated in school environments, however the sentiment is the same.

Consider your own daily experiences of shared understanding. This is commonly defined as an acknowledged set of systems and beliefs that do not require repetition but exist naturally in the daily work of the Deputy and Headteacher. In a study that viewed shared understanding through the lens of military coalitions, Smart et al. (2009) defined it as:

'...the ability of multiple agents to exploit common bodies of casual knowledge for the purpose of accomplishing shared goals' (Smart, 2009. p.9).

Expansion of this definition led them to identify four deeper meanings:

- **Identical:** understanding among all individuals within a specified task or area, irrespective of differences. It assumes that people understand things exactly the same way, especially when they have the same role in a specific job or task, e.g. everyone applying the exact same behaviour policy consistently across all areas of the school.

- **Similar:** centres on the similarities of abilities rather than absolute concurrence in understanding. Although individuals may not exhibit identical forms of understanding, they share similarities in their abilities, with variations in scope and depth.

- **Complementary:** people may contribute effectively to group tasks without having identical or similar skills. Applying skills that fit well with other group members, as seen in teams with specialised roles, e.g. English and science leads bringing different expertise to the school literacy strategy.

- **Distributed:** focuses on how different actions show understanding through various methods. It accepts that many ways can help us understand things, even letting machines be seen as understanding things in certain areas.

PERSONAL REFLECTION

Look at the types of shared understanding identified above, which have you experienced in your current role? Consider which type you could benefit from in your setting and the advantages of using a blended approach?

_____
_____
_____
_____

This book makes some use of business literature, unsurprisingly because schools, and MATs especially, are now medium to large scale businesses with budgets of millions of pounds, and hundreds of employees. This type of literature will always be helpful, but we find it intriguing to look to other areas of human interaction that require sacrifices and communication and, without being too much of a martyr, the military can provide this insight, to a degree. Smart et al. (2009), conclude that shared understanding can indeed contribute positively to what they call a coalition (very esoteric but not enough to alienate those of us for whom education often feels like our own battlefield) and how effective this is in creating organisational culture. We suggest that without shared understanding there cannot be an effective organisational culture.

Cultural alignment

It is unlikely that many Deputy Heads will be in a position to establish a culture or even a cultural tone within their school; even a Deputy Head of Culture and Behaviour will be ensuring fidelity to a culture and fealty to the Headteacher or leadership that set it. That is not to say there is no agency here, but Schein (2010) advocates that culture is always best when it is shared on a deeper level and this takes time, so Deputy Headteachers should be prepared to be flexible. Headteacher alignment might be something you are compromising some of your personal integrity for because you need the job or want stability. However, cultural differences are going to be harder to ignore and something that we recommend you investigate when applying for the job in the first place.

Nick Hart (2022), in his excellent book on school culture, speaks about Headteachers ensuring that language is shared in order for alignment to occur. The onus is on the Headteacher to ensure their vision has ease of alignment through the shared concepts outlined above.

Lack of alignment is different from conflict, however. Conflict with a leadership team is an essential test of trust and, as long as it is devoid of personal attacks and is centred around ideals and conceptual issues, conflict can be handled positively for the betterment of the school (Hart, 2022).

If you find yourself in a negative conflict or misalignment, here's what you could do.

DO	DO NOT
• Speak to your Headteacher about your concerns. • Make sure you are bringing solutions to your concerns, offering decent and sensible alternatives. • Ensure your solutions fall in line with the culture and ethos of your Headteacher.	• Attack your Headteacher's culture – this is something they are likely to have been working on for some time and whilst you might disagree, this isn't the time for personal attacks. • Presents problem X without solution Xi, Xii or Xiii as this will likely show your Headteacher that your lack of solution-focussed thinking means you might be less of a team player.

It is impossible to speak about the culture in schools without referencing Schein (2010) and his levels of organisational culture.

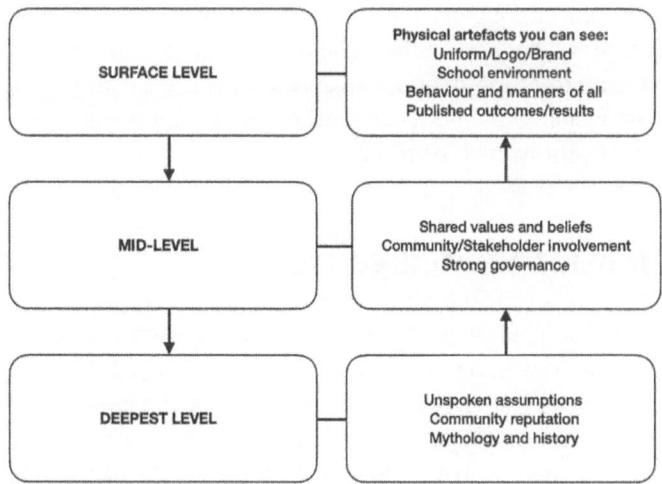

FIGURE 3: *The cycle of levels of culture, adapted from Ireland and Pattinson (2021)*

True success in culture can be measured in what people see and what people feel: *'This school feels really welcoming ... it's like a family ... you can really tell you're valued here'* are all examples of feedback from visitors to schools who just 'get' the school and its cultural intentions. Schein (2010) would say, and many more would agree, that this is because what is shown on the surface level can be traced back to a deeper, unspoken level of cultural understanding and alignment.

How many of us have encountered schools where changes to logo, uniform and behaviour policy hasn't yielded the expected end result of culture change? We would suggest that this is because the work hasn't been done on the deeper level of shared assumptions. Such work takes time to establish and requires buy-in from all stakeholders including the local community. The relationship between the levels is cyclical; the existence of one substantiates the other and your role in ensuring the continual evolution of the school culture will depend on the structure of your setting. Knowing the culture at the deepest level will require a close working relationship with your Headteacher: working towards this is one of your highest priorities.

Emotional intelligence

Emotional Intelligence (EI) is crucial for good leadership and organisational success (Goleman, 2000; Fullan, 2001). Many of the areas we have discussed require a certain level of EI in order to sensitively engage with them. If you want to refine your alignment with anyone in a close position of power, then your use of EI – and your understanding of their own capacity is essential; we call this 'concept of capacity'. It's about understanding the abilities and limits of the person you're working with.

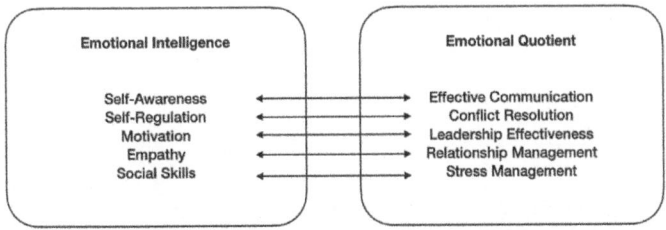

FIGURE 4: *Understanding the relationship between EI and EQ*

Consider Figure 4 and how each of our definitions of EI align with potential outcomes in your daily practice as a Deputy Head. Goleman (2009) said that effective leadership relies on how well leaders use their emotional intelligence to adapt to varying situations. Concept of capacity is a self-reflective and, perhaps, metacognitive skill not always naturally present in all leaders. Some of us need to actively work on these moments that require 360-degree reviews of your own practice or even a colour theory of personality such as 'Colour Works'. Whatever method you use, Miao et al. (2018)'s assertion that there is a 'conceptual overlap between EI and authentic leadership' (p.687) reinforces the absolute symbiotic nature of this relationship and is therefore ultimately worthy of your time and investment.

It's likely that you already have some awareness of your capacity, strengths and areas for growth. Take this opportunity to list moments of authentic leadership where your self-awareness and emotional intelligence have played a part.

Alignment heavily suggests the owner of this action will be making compromises and changing their own behaviour and expectations to match their Headteacher. Such chess-like movements are par for the course in the world of the Deputy

EMOTIONAL INTELLIGENCE	EMOTIONAL QUOTIENT	AUTHENTIC LEADERSHIP
Self-awareness	Effective communication	
Self-regulation	Conflict resolution	
Motivation	Leadership effectiveness	
Empathy	Relationship management	
Social skills	Stress management	

Head but, as Gwyn ap Hari so eloquently demonstrated, those without a sense of loyalty to the ethos and culture could end up destroying it.

Sometimes, we all 'fall in' and acquiesce to the company line when we may not agree with it. But isn't that the art of it all? Isn't it our job to not professionally embarrass our Head in the moment but to find the time to gently pull them to one side and professionally enquire into their reasoning or motives? You may well be told that *this is the way we're doing it,* or *I'm sorry but this needs to happen.* With your method of inquiry, you open yourselves up to the alignment that will secure the next step in the school's journey.

It's not quite as sycophantic as recent UK Government Cabinet 'collective responsibility', whereby a distinct difference in opinion would result in a resignation, but rather more like a supply shuttle docking with the International Space Station: small nudges, slight shifts of expectations and a secure and confident bond that ensure the survival of the good ship school. If you have found the Head with whom you can align causes little friction then you are among the blessed. However, if you find yourself in a position where compromise is too much, return to your sense of self – your concept of capacity – and analyse whether or not you can make the requisite changes to your leadership style to stay in place. The right Headteacher is out there for you, and they might just be the one you're struggling with.

Shaun Passey, of no relation and Subject Leader of Drama and Theatre Studies at a sixth form college said of prospective Deputy Headteachers:

> *'Many I have spoken to have found leading a subject area to be the sweet spot – it allows them to focus on what they love: their subject and the classroom. Moving up to Deputy Head is a different challenge altogether,*

and it requires being certain that you can align yourself with someone else's vision, bring it to fruition and carry the staff with you. It's one thing to drive change within a department, galvanizing a smaller team you know well. It's quite another to roll out whole-school approaches and persuade everyone to get on board – especially if your vision doesn't align with the Headteacher's. I imagine that kind of ideological conflict could be soul destroying. But at the end of the day, the head calls the shots. And that's that.'

Look to yourself, first and always.

2

Establishing and managing relationships

Deputy Heads often succeed where others may struggle because they are in a position that demands skills in first establishing and subsequently managing a multitude of relationships across countless situations and contexts. It seems to us that the best Deputy Heads do this by intimately understanding their own leadership approach through reflective practice and a sense of decency. Acting in a way that is morally right, fair and honest to everyone involved, with empathy influencing communication and authenticity.

If you are reflecting on yourself as a leader, then you first need to get to grips with leadership theory and its history.

A brief look at leadership theory

The 'nature versus nurture' debate often surfaces in discussions surrounding education, particularly in child psychology and development. While genetics undeniably plays a role in educational outcomes, the environment curated by educators can significantly influence and sometimes counteract these genetic predispositions (Thomas, 2018). The same debate extends into the realm of leadership, through Trait theory – the idea that leadership abilities are innate rather than developed. Yet for a Deputy Head, what's crucial is recognising that while some natural tendencies may exist, the vital skills for this role are largely cultivated and strengthened through deliberate practice.

Research shows that certain leadership traits provide a foundation, but the real measure of leadership comes from how these traits are applied and refined over time (Stodgill, 1974; Northouse, 2018). What this means for you: don't worry if you don't feel like a 'natural' leader. The skills that matter most in Deputy Headship – relationship building, strategic thinking and adaptive problem-solving – can all be developed.

As we explore the intersection of innate traits and learned behaviours in leadership, it is crucial to acknowledge the dynamic quality of leadership itself. The shift from genetic predispositions to behavioural and situational factors marks an important evolution in leadership theory, paving the way for a more nuanced understanding of what it takes to lead effectively.

Rather than focusing on *who* the leader is, Style theory considers what the leader does. Style theories emphasise that leadership effectiveness hinges not just on intrinsic traits but also on the adaptive choices leaders make in response to varying situations. Hoffman et al. (2011) bolstered the view that Trait theory remained relevant by demonstrating its impact on leadership effectiveness compared to skill-based approaches. However, if Trait theory is about nature and how you instinctively respond to things, then Style theories address nurture and the actions of an effective leader. Trent (2004) argues that leaders must adeptly navigate diverse scenarios, utilising various skills and adapting their approach to fit each unique context. This adaptability is viewed as a learned strength rather than a fixed trait.

As leadership theory evolved, it built upon earlier research to incorporate new insights into what makes leaders successful.

This evolution marks a shift from genetic theories to a more nuanced understanding of leader's behaviours and styles. Studies by Trent (2004) and Hoffman et al. (2011) explore different leadership styles, such as coercive, authoritative, affiliative, democratic, pacesetting, and coaching, each generating distinct outcomes based on the context and the leader's characteristics. Goleman (2000) further expands on this by framing leadership as fundamentally tied to emotional intelligence (EI).

As a writing pair, we met on the MA in Educational Leadership from the National Institute of Teaching and Education in 2021. Keen to learn about how to lead schools with people at the heart of the endeavour, we were both drawn to the structure of the course around the leadership of culture and people. Subsequently, we have strengthened our belief that relationships underpin the best leadership.

Hannah Abbiss is Deputy Head of a one form entry Church of England primary school in Wolverhampton and shares her experience of her evolving understanding of establishing relationships as a leader. Hannah's advice around relationship building is equally applicable to a secondary school context.

PROFESSIONAL PERSPECTIVE

By Hannah Abbiss – Deputy Head of St Albans C of E Primary, Wolverhampton

The Early Career Framework states: 'Building effective relationships is easier when pupils believe that their feelings will be considered and understood'. As a leader, however, there is no guidance. No framework for us. However, it is one of the most crucial traits to being a leader in schools.

I first started at my school as (what was then) a Recently Qualified Teacher and slowly progressed to becoming a phase leader, before moving on to become an Assistant Headteacher, and later the Deputy. For me, having been at the school for such a long time, I knew that building trust in my new role within the school community was paramount.

Relationships, in this sense, were not merely beneficial for the school; they were essential, certainly at the point that we were on our school's journey. As a teacher and as a leader, I have witnessed first-hand the impact that strong, positive relationships can have not only on staff morale, but also on children's outcomes.

When I initially transitioned into the role of Deputy Headteacher, I understood that my responsibility was not just to support the Headteacher, but to serve as a link between the school's staff and the Head. It was important to me that I was transparent with the staff: I was a new senior leader, I would be learning along the way, but I was there to listen, to support and to challenge. I aimed to develop the culture – something we often hear about but is not necessarily tangible – to ensure that staff felt valued, listened to and included.

My leadership choices reflected this: from the smaller points, such as saying good morning with a smile to people as they pass, to organising small Christmas gifts, to the consistent approach I took to developing the school and our staff. This style was also important when working alongside staff when developing curriculum and ensuring a 'done with' model was maintained at all times, giving staff ownership and confidence. Moreover, relationships with the pupil's parents were equally important. Engaging with families and understanding them and their children created a supportive network

> that was built through regular communication in the form of newsletters, face-to-face conversations, being present at the school gate every morning and evening, and participating in community events. This proactive approach not only strengthened our connections but also further developed a sense of belonging for our school community: we were all in this together.
>
> As the Deputy Headteacher, I have spent many years being the consistent face amongst many transitions that the school has faced. Each new appointment of Headteachers brought with it a unique set of challenges and expectations, and I had to ensure that staff did not feel uncertain or apprehensive about possible changes, to enabling our school community to adapt and continue to thrive. Each time there was a change in the school's leadership, I endeavoured to reassure our staff that while leadership may change, our core values remain the same. Funnily enough, many parents have asked me why I have never applied for the Headteacher role over the years, and, honestly, I wouldn't want to. As a teaching Deputy, I have the best of both worlds, and although busy and overwhelming most of the time, it gives me a sense of unity and compassion for all staff.

Hannah's perspective offers much for the successful Deputy Head to unpack and learn from. Perhaps the most significant aspect of how she sees Deputy Headship, and indeed leadership more generally, is her perception of strategic opportunities in the seemingly operational. 'Being on the school gate every morning and evening' is a task that sits on the checklist of most Deputy Heads and is usually seen as just that – a task. However, Hannah frames this as an opportunity to build relationships. Any leader who has made a habit of this practice will attest to the number of potential crises they have been able to resolve at the gate before they became something bigger.

Then there is the issue of change that Hannah identifies as something that Deputy Heads need to both absorb themselves and lead for others. This is often an underappreciated pressure, as Deputy Heads, need to adapt to the new scenarios while also reassuring others and showing them the way into the new shared reality. This is especially true in schools where there has been significant change. It is the Deputy Head's leadership, rooted in the trust of their colleagues, that lights the way. And, of course, authenticity must underpin trust.

Authentic leadership

The lead text of our Educational Leadership MA course was *Why Should Anyone Be Led by You?* by Goffee and Jones (2019). After years of extensive research across multiple sectors, this seminal work defines leadership through a statement: 'be yourself – more – with skill' (p.17). The issue here is that this means they are defining leadership through the lens of anyone who takes up the position, including their specific context, personality, private lives, personal belief systems, ethics and myriad other variables that arguably reduce their argument to being wholly subjective. Goffee and Jones emphasise behaviour and choice. If you are behaving in a manner informed by your assessment of the situation and making leadership choices that reflect this, delivering these choices with skill then you will be leading authentically and will more likely attract others who will follow your lead.

So, who is talking about authentic leadership? The issue is that many other words cloud the field. In 2024, former Headteacher and education consultant Tom Sherrington released a blog about a behaviour debate that had resurfaced online. The post, which focused on his insights into his own shortcomings as a leader, really struck a chord in the social media savvy education community. Comments centred around celebrating his vulnerability and that 'by allowing ourselves to assimilate our experiences through acknowledgement of errors and being of a mindset that allows growth, we cannot underestimate the positive impact this will have on our own leadership journeys and those of the people who follow us' (Passey, 2024).

What does it mean, to be authentic and how can you link this to successfully establishing and managing relationships in leadership? Lehman et al. (2019) said that 'authenticity references

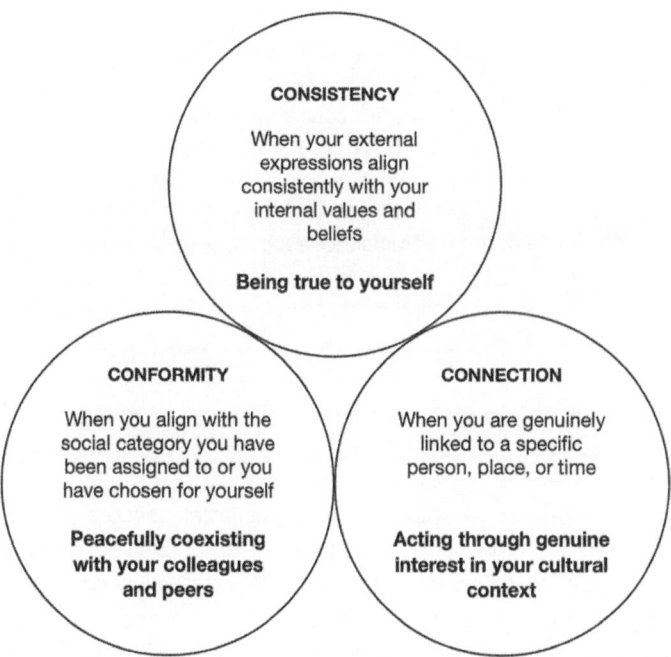

FIGURE 5: *Multiplicity of Authenticity Definitions, adapted from Lehman et al. (2019)*

the intangible' (p. 21) and propose that whilst authenticity relies on honesty and truth, a definition is hard to come by. If we presume that authenticity relies on being yourself with more skill and adapting to each circumstance and context, how can it be defined by static maxims such as 'real, genuine or true' (pg. 21)? To help, Lehman et al. conceived of three meanings of leadership that combine to a notion of authenticity: see figure 5.

You can begin to assess your own sense of authenticity through the lenses of consistency, conformity and connection. If you are struggling to connect authentically with a situation or person, you may be lacking in one of the areas.

> **PERSONAL REFLECTION**
>
> Considering the ideas of consistency, connection and conformity, can you think of a time where you were successful in navigating one or more of these in a new setting? You might even want to draw the three circles and find different examples for each.

In Chapter 1, we explored emotional intelligence and how this can be developed through your emotional awareness and ability to adapt your day-to-day work to align with your Headteacher. Using this as a starting point to assess your own sense of authenticity in your school may give you a much better chance of establishing authentic relationships and managing and nurturing them as they evolve within your context.

ESTABLISHING AND MANAGING RELATIONSHIPS

With the educational landscape constantly shifting and evolving, stakeholders (and how you interact with them) can appear dramatically different depending on the makeup and design of your school. Some Deputy Heads may rarely have the chance to influence such forward-facing policies and experiences whereas others may very well crave the protection of an office space.

The word 'stakeholder' is not our first choice of word to describe a person or group of people who are an important and indispensable part of your school community. We use this word, however, because rather than 'supporter' or 'community member', our chosen descriptor helps highlight the reciprocal nature of the relationship: they have a vested interest in the school's success and this should be recognised.

Broadly speaking, there are several key stakeholders that appear for most schools and educational settings, as in Figure 6:

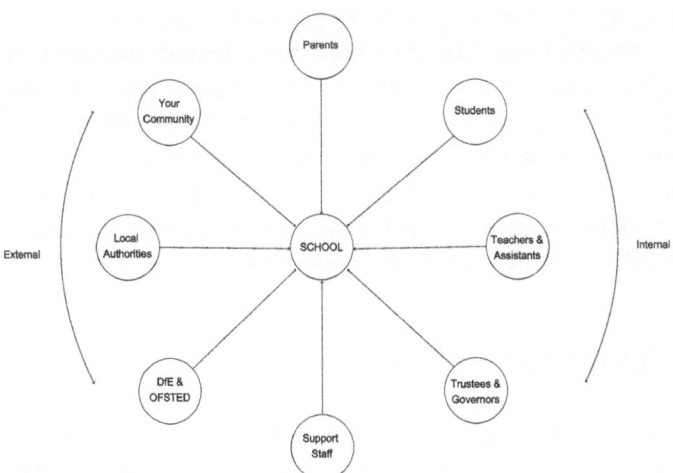

FIGURE 6: *Key stakeholders in schools*

The smooth running of any organisation is achieved through robust and deep relationships with a wide range of stakeholders.

When first introduced to school settings as a peripatetic music teacher, an incredibly dear friend said: 'if you want to get on here, make friends with the receptionist'. What he had hit upon wasn't just a way of calming nerves or even ensuring a car parking space at 8:34am on a Tuesday to teach five-year-olds how to sing *'one, two, three: it's good to be me'*. Instead, Richard Skilbeck, now Director of Music and Assistant Head of Sixth Form at Edgbaston High School for Girls, had revealed a truth that would be written about in an education book some twenty years later. There are people in a school that are not the Head or Deputy, but quiet observers of the daily goings on of the school in all its glorious ways and they are just as important as those who run the school. Richard teaches us that humility in the role, and not assuming the power of your place in the arbitrary hierarchy, is one of the keys to successfully leading people with diverse personality types and situations.

Those of you who may have risen through the ranks of school leadership in a more orthodox manner will recognise this generous nod to the gatekeepers of our schools and beyond. Making an active choice to connect with and engage in the culture, time and place of your setting – including all of its stakeholders – will embed you further in your school and establish stronger working relationships.

How this can help

With so many different personalities, backgrounds and personal requirements inherent within a school community, we offer some strategies to help you consider the power imbalances that naturally come with your role:

Problem solving

Build trust and rapport

Your ability, and opportunity, to establish trust and support are crucial for navigating power imbalances. Prioritise building a positive working relationship based on mutual respect, open communication and collaboration. Actively listening to concerns and perspectives demonstrates your personal reliability and professionalism. This could allow you to seek future opportunities to support leadership and school-wide initiatives in building and growing culture in your setting.

Understand the stakeholder's priorities

In the face of ever-increasing workload and responsibilities, it's important to try and gain deeper insight into your stakeholders' priorities and goals. You may even be able to determine their leadership style (perhaps unknown to them) and how you can adapt to it. By attempting to understand the personal and professional motivations behind their decision making, and therefore how they prefer to operate, it's possible to tailor your approach to align with your stakeholder's motives while still advocating for your own perspectives on issues that matter to you. This demonstrates a willingness to support their position while also contributing valuable insights from your perspective.

Choose the right time and place

Timing is everything, right? So, when advocating for your perspective, try to choose the right time and place to engage in a potentially controversial interaction. Avoid confrontation in public spaces or during moments of palpable tension or stress. Your job isn't to add to their worries or concerns, and so your engagement in serious conversation needs to be carefully timed. For example, having just had the Ofsted call is not the time to begin challenging the Headteacher's decisions around the appointment of subject leaders. This ability to choose your moments, demonstrates sensitivity and professionalism and could increase the likelihood of a positive outcome.

Present solutions, not just problems

Having sworn by this method since day one, we can attest to the power of solution-focused problem solving. If you are raising concerns or advocating for alternative perspectives, always come prepared with potential solutions and alternative suggestions. Instead of immediately identifying flaws and issues, try to offer constructive suggestions for improvement that demonstrates your proactive approach to problem solving. Your aim is to demonstrate initiative and a commitment to finding mutually beneficial outcomes for all parties.

Examples of this might be:

- Conducting a policy review and presenting a revised version incorporating feedback from teachers, students, and parents, along with a plan for implementation and evaluation

- Creating a methodology in support of a proposed new approach to a current monitoring system that staff have voiced concerns about.

Frame discussions in terms of school improvement

Make clear that your perspective is framed in terms of school improvement and student success. Your stakeholders will have these aims at the heart of their progression plans and tying your ideas into these will allow negotiating space. Emphasising how your proposed initiatives align with the school's goals and mission, and highlighting the benefits for students, staff and wider stakeholders will contribute to the potential success of your contributions. This is collaboration and consensus building in action.

Be persistent, yet patient

There will always be a power imbalance between you and those without the authority of your position and this is to be embraced, not challenged, for effective teams. Navigating this whilst advocating for change within any hierarchical structure takes time and persistence. You should be prepared to engage in ongoing dialogue and negotiation with your stakeholders, for example, recognising that meaningful change may well require incremental progress over time. Staying focussed on long term goals and remaining patient and resilient in the face of challenges and setbacks will result in effective negotiation of power imbalances.

Conflict resolution

Diplomatic, collaborative and strategic approaches to resolve conflict will always be better than a spirited and ill thought out confrontation, but this isn't always possible. Time is not in the gift of many teachers and educators, with directed time being statutorily set for most schools. Therefore, the ability to resolve conflict and address disagreements constructively is crucial for maintaining – and modelling – positive relationships and promoting effective collaboration within a school system.

Here are some practical strategies you might consider employing if you find yourself in a situation where challenge seems necessary yet not without risk:

Create a safe environment for dialogue

Do what you can to create an environment where open communication between you and your stakeholders is encouraged and where you both feel safe to express your thoughts and concerns. Emphasise the importance of respectful communication, encouraging it with ground rules for a constructive dialogue such as active listening. This might include paraphrasing what the other person has said in order to check your understanding overtly. This helps to avoid personal attacks and helps keep the focus on issues rather than individuals.

Practise active listening

Actively listening to the perspectives of all parties involved in the discussion will demonstrate your empathy and an ability to paraphrase and summarise their viewpoints to ensure clarity and show that you are genuinely engaged in the conversation. Obviously, you should avoid interrupting or dismissing others and actively strive to understand the concerns expressed and the underlying motives behind their perspective.

Clarify misunderstandings

Often, conflicts arise due to misunderstandings or miscommunications. To avoid this, take proactive steps to clarify everyone's understanding of the situation by asking questions that seek clarification and confirming your own misunderstandings of the presented perspective. By addressing these issues directly, you can prevent conflicts from escalating and allow all parties to identify and reach a common ground more easily.

Here are some conversation starters and phrases we have found useful:

- Addressing misunderstandings:
  I think I may have misunderstood your point – can you clarify for me?
  Let's make sure we're not missing anything important here. Can you talk me through your understanding of it again?

- Confirming understanding:
  Let me repeat that back to you so you can make sure I've understood
  If I've understood correctly, you are suggesting that ...

- Seeking clarification
  Can you help me understand what you meant by...
  I want to make sure I understand correctly. Are you saying that...?

- Finding common ground:
  It sounds like we both agree on... Is that right?
  Let's focus on the points we both agree on ...

Focus on interests, not positions

You are all there (hopefully!) for the right reasons (although of course, these reasons will be different from person to person). The betterment of life chances for young people is what drives leaders and it is in these motives that we can find a common ground. Focussing on these rather than entrenched beliefs about the most appropriate actions is a far more productive way to resolve conflict. Once a shared mission has been reaffirmed, you can productively and calmly negotiate the particulars around the best way to pursue this mission. You are in the perfect position to assist others in identifying their underlying needs, concerns and priorities thereby exploring potential solutions that address them. It's this reframing of the conversation, in terms of shared goals and interests, that fosters collaboration and enables mutually beneficial solutions.

Workshop potential solutions

You're a born problem solver so why not use those skills here? Engage, as much as you can, in a collaborative mind mapping process that tries to generate a range of potential solutions to the conflict presented to you. If you actively encourage creativity and innovation through exploring various options and alternatives – even if they seem impractical or unconventional – you can increase buy-in and commitment to the eventual solution.

Seek compromise and win-win solutions

Compromise is the artform in question here, and you must be the master of it as a Deputy Head. In striving to find compromise and win-win solutions that – if you're lucky – address the needs and concerns of all parties involved, you will be demonstrating and encouraging flexibility, as well as a willingness to make concessions in pursuit of a mutually satisfactory outcome. If done well, you will embody the value of collaboration and cooperation in achieving long-term goals and maintaining positive relationships.

Use 'I' statements and non-defensive communication

We think there is a strength of confidence in an informed opinion. When expressing your own perspective or concern, the strong use of 'I' statements to establish ownership of your thoughts and feelings without implicating or blaming others is of huge benefit. You can practise non-defensive communication by remaining calm, composed and open to feedback even in the face of criticism or disagreement. By modelling constructive communication techniques to those around you, you can set a positive example for them and encourage a more collaborative approach to conflict resolution.

Constructive communication techniques might include:

- Active listening: asking clarifying questions to register that you are engaged (see page 48).
- Being clear and direct with instructions to avoid misunderstandings: *'We need x by this specified time'*.
- Framing feedback positively: *'what went well, even better if...'*
- Monitoring body language, tone of voice and eye contact and adapting where appropriate to fit with the context.

Follow up and reflect

Once a resolution has been reached, make the effort to follow up with all parties involved to ensure that the agreed-upon solution is implemented effectively and to address any remaining concerns or issues. You should also make time to reflect on the conflict resolution process, identifying lessons learned and areas for improvement for all concerned. Use the feedback processes from this experience to refine your future approach to conflicts and continue building a culture of open communication and constructive conflict resolution within the school leadership team and the wider community.

Find strength in authenticity

Assuming all is well because the waters are calm around the swan is to ignore the ferocity with which the animal is swimming. If authenticity is the key, then so is adaptability and the only thing that follows that is exhaustion. Being true to yourself by allowing vulnerability and honesty to be worn like your heart on a chainmail sleeve is not an easy feat.

It is far too easy for others to disregard your authenticity as weakness. Phrases like *'this is just a job', 'I'll only work the hours I'm paid'* speak to a nervousness around the idea of vulnerability. But none of our advice, and none of the job, can be achieved successfully from behind a protective screen.

Yet is it within the virtues of authentic leadership that we find the solution to the exhaustion of adaptability: just be honest.

CASE STUDY: STUART

Yesterday, Stuart received news that would fundamentally change his afternoon: a serious safeguarding concern that required immediate action. The meeting was scheduled for 10:05am exactly, conflicting with his Year 10 Maths lesson.

The meeting concluded with a list of significant actions required before the end of the school day. Stuart faced a

ESTABLISHING AND MANAGING RELATIONSHIPS

> choice: hide his emotional response or acknowledge the impact while maintaining professional effectiveness.
>
> The meeting ends and Stuart sinks into his chair.
>
> As he exits the office he is greeted by a passing member of staff who comments on his gaunt and angry appearance.

Unfortunately, these types of situations are ever-increasing but they are ones we must all face as leaders. What does Stuart do here? Clearly, he's angry and disgusted at the appalling situation but he can't let that show, can he? How unprofessional, surely. This is correct, to a degree. Whilst it is part of the role of leadership not to let the stresses of the day influence your interactions with students and staff, an authentic leader might take a moment to inform those around them of their mindset appropriately.

The following is a real example of a statement made in a staff room that yielded incredibly positive responses from those in accidental coffee consuming attendance.

> Stuart chose authenticity with boundaries. In the staffroom, he said: *'I wanted to let you know I'm dealing with a serious safeguarding matter today. You might notice I seem focused elsewhere – it's not about anything you've done, and I'm managing it appropriately.'*

Stuart's approach acknowledged his human response to a real-life challenge, prevented staff from misreading his demeanour, maintained appropriate confidentiality and demonstrated that leaders can be both professional and human. His colleagues were given context surrounding Stuart's situation that day. They could then choose how to respond or adapt to the situation. Your authenticity will ring true with the people who can empathetically act to help you. The mantra of 'it's OK not to be OK' works quite well here because if you've spent the time establishing and maintaining relationships, then you will be fortunate enough to lean on these when needed.

Anecdotally, providing students with an appropriate version of the above statement can also prove fruitful. Students can tell when you're physically there in the room but not present. They'll feel the frustration redirected at them but won't necessarily be aware of the perpetrator or system that has riled you. Handled sensitively, even your students will benefit from your authenticity. Let's not forget Goffee and Jones' (2019) assertion that to be authentic is to be yourself with more skill. How can we apply that to Stuart's situation? When Stuart leaves his office, he is enraged and exhausted which, for any school setting, is a negative energy to be portrayed in the busy corridors or at break or lunchtime. Instead, Stuart could have gone through the following process, using his emotional intelligence to successfully identify parts of his personality that are beneficial to him.

- As our introductory contributor, Sally Alexander, often says with love and respect, 'check your face'. Take a moment to bring your awareness to how you look and what demeanour you will portray in your setting.

- You can't hide everything, so what skill do you have right now that can help? List making? Delegation? Is there something someone else could do that might help?

- What are your strengths, and which one of them can you employ now? If it's teaching and learning, why not begin a personal thought experiment about your next lesson?

- To not shy away from the severity of the situation, one of your skills might be the meticulous planning you do in order to keep your students safe. What room will you keep them in? Who will supervise and what will they be told? What will the parents be told and who will deliver the news to them? All of this may, depending on your sense of self, be a useful way of channelling your intense and understandable emotions

- Leave your room with purpose: drive towards your goal – next lesson, break duty – while remaining true to your authenticity of connection. Pick up litter as you go and complement good behaviour. Presenting and 'being' the energy you wish to see in the school is a good focus if your mind is frazzled and all you want to do is cry.

Authentic leaders care deeply

This job isn't for everyone and neither should it be. Very often SLT are the joke in a TikTok video, wearing hi-vis jackets and bedecked in far more lanyards than anyone needs. The best teams can be led by authentic leaders who care deeply about their school but who also use their authenticity to their advantage, and why can't that be you?

Your authenticity is your strength here: moments of *'I'm a little overwhelmed at the moment, but I acknowledge this conversation needs to happen, when are you free?'* are surely preferable to *'no, I'm not free. Ask Steven when my diary is clear.'* What you think you may lose from your protective armour of faux-professionalism you will almost certainly gain in respect and time.

Communication is key and, as with Stuart's face, much of this is silent. Renowned orchestral conductor Keith Slade said to us:

> 'The essence of conducting, in my opinion, is the art of drawing the best out of the ensemble and the music through creating an environment for musicians to flourish. Always being authentic and sharing a little of yourself helps hugely with the rapport a conductor builds with an orchestra. Engaging with people, whether it be the audience or performers, is vital to creating a memorable performance.'

If he can silently lead sixty people through emotional and musical journeys by forging a vocabulary that they all need to understand then it follows that you can bring your team together and teach them how you communicate success and failure, how you portray positive emotions and what you present when you need help.

In our next chapter on building trust and setting standards, we look more in depth at modelling vulnerability and authenticity. For now though, embrace being yourself and use all facets of your skills and personality to navigate the choppy waters of the job. A positive and successful school culture will follow.

3

Building trust and setting standards

As the Deputy Head, you are uniquely positioned to detect slipping standards that will need resetting. You are likely to be in and out of classrooms, communicating with pupils, performing break duties and corridor patrols and on the gate at the beginning and end of the day, witnessing countless interactions between staff and pupils, some focused on learning, others on behaviour and attitudes. 'Consistency and coherence at a whole-school level are paramount' (Education Endowment Foundation, 2021) and when the focus and consistency dip, you'll sense it.

Try looking out for the following cues and signs:

- Inconsistent applications of uniform and behaviour policies, which may well begin in the classroom or corridors with staff
- Inconsistency in the language used by staff during key routines
- Expectations on the behaviour basics (such as moving around the building) starting to slip
- Teachers assuming that 'it's been taught so they'll have learned it' instead of engaging in the rigour of consistently checking student understanding

> **PERSONAL REFLECTION**
>
> What other signs can you think of that might indicate a slipping of standards?
>
> _____
> _____
> _____
> _____
> _____

You are the ideal person to reset standards, however, you walk a delicate line between being the person to set the reminder about standards and being seen as someone who seems obsessed with compliance and uniformity, waiting to catch out anyone who dips ever so slightly beneath the pedantically compliant. Does it really matter if there is a little bit of chat while they get on with their work? Is it the end of the world if they're slightly boisterous in the corridor the week before the end of term? Yes, those shirts are starting to be untucked more often than not but are we seriously saying that has an impact on what they learn? The short answer is that yes, it matters. It matters a great deal because standards set the tone for the culture and ethos of a school.

How do you maintain the trust of those whose standards you are often having to reset? This gets explored in depth later and we suggest that rather than always acting on popular opinion, consistency is the preferable approach. 'Consistency ensures that teachers are calm and in control' (McVey, 2020), and this feeling of calm begins from the consistency of the leaders. Teachers need to know what to expect and what is important and know that it is so every day. Only then can they reach the point of calm whereby they can pass on the same

BUILDING TRUST AND SETTING STANDARDS

immovable expectations to pupils. People trust the predictable and that is why you must be resolute in your commitment to the standards your school insists upon. Your integrity – 'having strong moral principles that you refuse to change' (Cambridge Dictionary, 2024) – is your key to bridging the paradox between setting the highest standards and maintaining the trust of others.

Another useful tool is delegation. It's satisfying being in a leadership position and discovering that the commitment to seemingly small key standards and values really do help achieve wider goals. As middle leaders, we recall being tasked with developing a more positive reading culture across the school and suddenly the importance of form tutors checking daily that all students had a reading book with them as well as one on their own desk presented itself to us

As the Deputy Head, the important thing here is to be the leader who supports others through this realisation. Be there to help them reflect and identify the shift in their own understanding but don't make them confront their earlier ignorance – the likelihood is that they are already doing that for themselves. It is, however, important to check that this is indeed the case and address the situation if it is not. That is part of the reflective conversation you should help them to have. You want to know if they have recognised the mistake and the lessons they intend to take from it. Telling them the mistake won't give you this vital information. Presenting them with different perspectives and evidence, and guiding them to reflect on this, is far more likely to make a lasting change.

Setting standards while also building trust is a fine balance. However, rather than seeing them as two opposing sides of the same coin, success rests on developing an understanding that they are mutually useful. You can reset standards much more efficiently and widely when you have trust, and it is far easier to develop trust when you are resolutely loyal to your standards.

Model vulnerability

One of the reasons that adults in school may have difficulty establishing a trusting relationship with the Senior Leadership Team (SLT), particularly the Deputy Head, is that vulnerability is often perceived as the preserve of those in the classroom. We are all likely to have worked with a senior leader who spends a lot of their time telling others where they are going wrong but has never been seen in a classroom and rarely receives feedback from observers. This is not an issue for education alone. Development Dimensions International (DDI) recently found that '32% of people say that they trust senior leaders in their organisations' and 'People were 5.3 times more likely to trust leaders who showed vulnerability' (DDI, 2023).

According to *Harvard Business Review* (Omadeke, 2022), sharing personal experiences and moments of vulnerability can help leaders connect more deeply with their teams and build trust through authenticity. We propose that trust is virtually impossible to cultivate if there is no shared experience upon which it can be based. What Omadeke terms 'professional confessions' are crucial to this. It is all very well saying to people, *'I'm in your classrooms to help develop you, not to judge'* or *'I'm sitting in on this meeting so I can help you improve'* but without ever modelling the vulnerability that these situations produce, it is impossible to expect others to trust your motives. Place yourself in the position of vulnerability, model how you want people to deal with it, and it is highly likely that you will supercharge trust. Passey (2025) points out that vulnerability encompasses both tangible (physical weakness, environmental risk and professional instability) and intangible elements (emotional openness, trust over hope and, a willingness to take risks) and that sharing this amongst your teachers and wider

BUILDING TRUST AND SETTING STANDARDS

school community can foster positive relationships and build trust (Jopling and Zimmerman, 2023).

PERSONAL REFLECTION

Create a list of the qualities of the leaders you have worked with. Can you pinpoint the qualities of those who gained more respect and those who were less successful?

_____
_____
_____
_____
_____

Read the following case study and then reflect on this idea in relation to your current role.

CASE STUDY: ANITA

Meet Deputy Head of Professional Development, Anita. She has read extensively around instructional coaching (see Chapter 6) and she is excited to introduce it to her school. Her Headteacher is also enthusiastic but has not invested the time in understanding the research base or the differences between various types of coaching. Because Anita wants to create a more developmental culture, she decides that every teacher who has been teaching for more than three years should be a coach. She recognises the training needs that this model carries, yet she is confident that the payoff will be significant.

Initially, Anita decides to provide a crib sheet of 'how to run a coaching session' and source videos from the internet to exemplify each part of the crib sheet. She then plans to observe coaching sessions during departmental time and provide feedback to the coaches. However, having run this idea past a colleague, and heard their concerns about staff being observed without first having time to practise in a low stake environment, she has a re-think. Anita's aim is to engender a developmental culture within the teaching team. For this to happen, she needs people to embrace their development areas and create psychological safety around the idea of not being an expert at something straight away.

Anita decides that instead of her original plan, she will run four training sessions on how to carry out coaching observations and run coaching conversations. During each session, she decides to use a video of herself either teaching or coaching. Each session explores a different aspect of the coaching process, using Anita's videos as a reflection point. Anita thinks that this will be valuable during the session in identifying the most high-leverage next step for a teacher because the whole team will be watching a video of her teaching and identifying the areas she should focus on next.

Throughout the four sessions, the conversation becomes increasingly open, with some staff members even volunteering aspects of their practice that they find the most challenging. Others ask questions about the coaching process that they admit they might have felt 'silly' asking before. The feedback at the end of the four sessions is that staff are excited to get started with instructional coaching and, crucially, not afraid to ask for help if they need it.

Enable reflection

Before offering substantive moments of reflection, use your leadership position to reflect on your own development. Using a tool to measure vulnerability is an excellent method. Figure 7 illustrates one way in which asking these questions about a specific situation – a moment of evaluation – will not only assess the adaptive capacity of the leader but will also model vulnerability to a staff body if used as an example in a staff briefing or PD session.

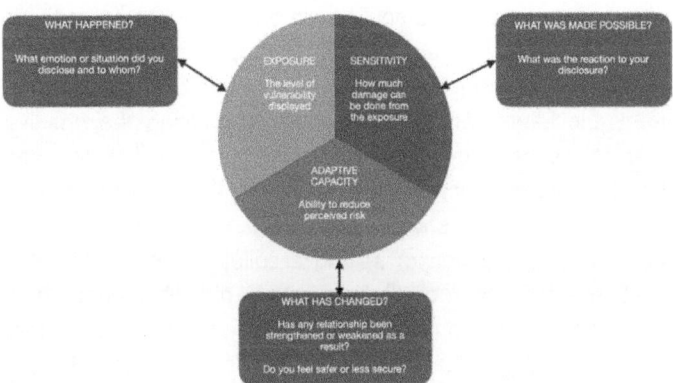

FIGURE 7: *Self-reflection into vulnerability for teachers (Passey, 2025)*

Once vulnerability has been modelled (for example, a leader teaching a lesson and being honest enough to share that it didn't go as planned) it will become a powerful culture driver, especially if it is cultivated regularly. As with anything in school leadership, keeping it relevant once it is initially launched is perhaps the most difficult. Yet, as a concept, keeping things relevant seems so simple. The Deputy Head who makes space for continued opportunities to talk about vulnerability will find greater trust is created as a result. Enabling people to reflect on the learning they have taken from their vulnerable moment will help them focus on what to change next time and therefore how to improve. As your culture of vulnerability spreads, progress and improvement will become things that people strive to achieve, free from the fear of judgement.

Enabling reflection can be as simple as asking someone how it went. When you know that someone you manage has shown vulnerability in a recent situation, pause and ask them how it went and what the outcome was. It will help them refocus on the positive impact of their vulnerability. If you feel it's appropriate, you could even pre-arrange to meet them after their vulnerable episode. For example, agreeing to meet a teacher who is having a group of teachers come to observe them and learn from their practice. Multiplying the positive interactions that surround a vulnerable episode is likely to mean that the person is increasingly comfortable with vulnerability.

The final thing to say on reflection is that when you are in the privileged position of seeing a colleague in a vulnerable position – in a corridor dealing with a difficult student or a classroom where you are the observer – keep in mind that your role is to use that vulnerability to develop that colleague and remind them that without it, they cannot improve. Vulnerability is a teacher's biggest asset, not because it reveals your weaknesses and thereby enables an evaluation of your base standard, but because by assuming vulnerability *without judgement,* you enable a mindset shift based on trust.

That leads us to the next aspect of trust development – delegation. Delegating aspects of your role that are important (though crucially not single points of failure), is a powerful way to show others that you trust them and their abilities. This is not the same thing as palming off all the parts of your role that you don't like doing. Enabling someone you line manage to have a go, under your watchful eye, at doing something just slightly beyond their current responsibility level that will allow them to grow, shows an investment in that person that is the bedrock of trust. You are backing them to succeed; they have your faith in them.

> **PERSONAL REFLECTION**
>
> Think about an upcoming conversation that you could use to help a colleague reflect on their performance and make improvements. Script out the parts of the conversation that you want to break the conversation into and add the reflection questions you will use.
>
> Alternatively, consider a recent conversation that you would like to revisit or that you could have approached differently.

Delegation in building trust

You can't do it all, and even if you could, it wouldn't be desirable. Even the most highly skilled Deputy Headteacher in charge of teacher development cannot build and sustain the same level of momentum for improvement that effective delegation creates. One of the greatest challenges in leadership is creating buy-in: a collective willingness to accept and actively participate in something. John Kotter famously created his 8-step model for change and wrote that 'whenever some minimum mass is not achieved early in the effort, nothing much worthwhile will happen' (Kotter, 1996). In your efforts to implement your teacher development programme, it is essential that you receive early support from within the team and one effective way to achieve this is through the delegation of responsibility for the programme's success. Take the example of instructional coaching: by identifying and carefully training a group of coaches from within the staff team, at the point of full roll out, not only did Anita have a group of coaches in a position to deliver better quality coaching and therefore increase the likelihood of success, but she also had a group of people with a vested interest in the success of a programme and therefore increased motivation to make it work. Furthermore, with a team of people echoing your key messages, any resistance is immediately placed against a team of voices rather than just your own. The strength that this adds to the message makes it all the more likely that others will trust the process and follow your lead.

Kotter (1996) also identified the danger of 'undercommunicating the vision'. Large-scale change can only take place when the vast majority of people are willing to make short-term sacrifices to their existing way of working in pursuit of a common goal. This reminds us that the delegation of responsibility for some aspects of teacher development will only be successful if the principles by which each delegated team member works are aligned. It may be helpful to consider principles through two different lenses: pedagogy and leadership.

Consider a middle leadership team made up of Heads of Department. As the teacher development lead, the Deputy Headteacher knows that they would like all department heads to explore the effectiveness of checking for understanding within their departments. The first challenge you face is to unite a shared understanding of what checking for understanding entails, when it is most effectively used and the questions that teachers should ask themselves when making decisions about how to check for understanding. Each Head of Department will bring the disciplinary requirements of their subject domain to that conversation so, in order to create alignment, you need to remain focused on the pedagogical principles of checking for understanding and allow the Heads of Department to consciously apply these in their own context.

Secondly, there is the leadership lens. What are your leadership principles and how can you engage each of the Heads of Department with them and ensure that they are applying them consistently when they work with colleagues in their departments? One important factor is being clear and tangible about what your principles are. At Birkbeck Primary school, our leadership principles are: decency, authenticity, rigour and development. The question that each Head of Department needs to carefully consider for delegation to be successful is, how do I apply those principles in my communication with my team, in what I ask of them and in how I train them?

As the leader, if you can create alignment of principles through the lenses of pedagogy and leadership, you will go a good deal of the way to ensuring that your delegation of the ongoing leadership of these areas can be effective because the fidelity to the original message, including the need for, aims of and vision for change, will remain high.

Values-based leadership

Peregrym and Wollf define values-based leadership as 'consistently leading out of personal values that are both desirable and beneficial for ourselves, those in our communities, and/or the organisations we serve' (2013, p.7). When people see that a leader makes decisions and takes actions that are easily linked back to their values and beliefs, this helps to create trust. It shows people that, where possible, you are considered and where you need to be, reactive, there will be fidelity to those principles, which helps others to understand your decisions and trust that your reaction will not be dictated by an emotional response. You will not be someone who changes your expectations of others from one day to the next, based on your mood that day. Schools are complex and dynamic places and over time, values may change through necessity or choice. However, when this happens, be open and deliberate about it so that others have a clear sense of what to expect and what is expected of them. Anyone who has worked in schools for any length of time can attest to the value of consistency in the behaviour of leaders. This is not to say that you will never have a bad day or be in a bad mood. You will, but when this happens, you must take measures to ensure that this does not influence how you treat others or, crucially, what you expect of them. This must always be rooted in your values.

In her book, *Dare to Lead*, Professor Brené Brown wrote about the importance of really knowing what you stand for (2018). This is because you can't (for any significant length of time), fake it. Building on the example from the previous section, you can't keep up the pretence of being all about vulnerability if you go to great lengths to avoid it yourself, for example. As Brown put it, you need to 'walk your talk' (Brené Brown, 2018). By doing so, you begin to exude an element of consistency. People know where they stand with you and they know what to expect. If you are public and overt about your values, they will even begin to know what you will expect of them. It is extremely empowering to know that you are free to make decisions you feel are best in any given moment, as long as those decisions link back to an agreed upon or expected value. It provides a psychological safety that frees people from worry and anxiety about making mistakes. Your values, when modelled and openly discussed, are one of your greatest tools in your quest to develop trust. As we shall see, they are also extremely useful in helping you to set standards and as such, a crucial tool in bridging the central paradox from the start of this chapter. Passey (2024) spoke about the difficulty of defining vulnerability through the lens of educational leadership but that we also know that trust is a crucial fact in enhancing relational reciprocity (Bruni and Tufano, 2017; Kleynhans et al., 2022) and so we should be feeding these into our values – and leadership styles – as much as we can.

PERSONAL REFLECTION

What are the values that you want to lead with? To what extent are they aligned with the leadership values of your Headteacher?

_____
_____
_____
_____
_____

Consistency is the key

Consistency is the quality that characterises the highest standards. Being great on the day is all well and good but it is what you do day in, day out that really shows how high your standards are. This is also where your values become the heartbeat of the standards you set. If you claim to be all about rigour, how consistently is that demonstrated? If you truly value development, how consistently do you apply that particular value?

CASE STUDY: JO

Rigour is a value that I have personal experience with, having worked with Deputy Head, Jo, for three years. Jo's commitment to seeing things through 'in their entirety' typifies her leadership and left me, as her Assistant, with no room for uncertainty about what was expected. This is not to say that we valued all of the same things. Although we were both driven by doing the best for the children at the forefront of our minds, there were certainly other things about which we disagreed. However, I always knew what was expected and that was because I saw it in her, every second of every day. She would pick up any stray piece of backing paper and would never let a child run past her in the corridor without having to turn around, go back to their starting point and walk. I never once saw her miss a deadline or produce a report that wasn't thorough and complete.

It sent a message to me, and to everyone else, that rigour was important to her and even though her expectations were at times, dare I say, beyond the reach of some of us at that time, she was consistent and I never felt any sense of judgement. To be clear, I am not saying that every leader should be like Jo. What I am saying, though, is that when you decide on what your values are, be consistent with them.

Consistency makes you predictable in a positive sense. It enables others to be in no doubt about where the standards are and, crucially with our paradox in mind, it enables them to trust your motives. Being true to your values drives both standards and trust and in doing so, helps us bridge our paradox.

> **PERSONAL REFLECTION**
>
> Think of a leader you have worked with who clearly showed their values. What were those values and how did being consistent with them affect others?
>
> _____
> _____
> _____
> _____
> _____

When standards slip

Standards slipping is painfully inevitable at certain times. The trick is to spot that slippage immediately. For example, when student uniforms become noticeably sloppier, this needs to be noticed, and as leaders, we need to step in.

When standards do slip, as they inevitably will from time to time, your values will once again be the thing you fall back on. Consider the difference between telling someone you'd like them to pay closer attention to the uniform standards in their classes at the start and end of lessons and asking them if they feel they are showing as much fidelity to the value of rigour in the context of uniform expectations as they could be. Instead of the reminder being about uniform, it has been reframed to be about the consistent application of a shared value. You will have also negated the person's internal response 'does it really matter?' because it is not the uniform itself that matters, but rather the consistent application of the value of rigour, and the uniform is a symptom of that.

Pupil needs as the driver

For some, this section might trigger memories of senior leaders justifying any unreasonable demands on staff or effectively ending any debate with 'we're doing it because it's best for the students'. While this may have been the case in theory, it effectively puts a stop on any debate which enables senior leaders to avoid the vulnerability of having to explain and justify their decisions. So, readers will be relieved to know that this is not what we mean by this heading.

Instead, we propose that the starting point for any change implementation plan should be pupil needs. As a Deputy Head, you will be responsible for implementing changes that inevitably impact the working days of countless staff members. The positive impact on students is generally worth the effort it takes to embed new changes. To achieve this, begin every change process by considering what the students' needs are and how you know them. Look beyond data headlines, as often there will be a delay in the reality of student experience being seen by this metric. Conduct purposeful student voice (interviews to find out the views of students on a specific issue), speaking to students about their experiences in lessons, the thinking that they do during instruction and the understanding they have taken as a result. Look for patterns in their behaviours in lessons and around school and once you think you have spotted something consistent, test it out over a longer period.

Driving change as a direct response to student needs mitigates any risk of the leader seemingly changing things for their personal motivations. Sometimes, we might hear staff comment, 'Oh, that's his thing' or even, 'That project is her baby'. Not always, but these kinds of comments can be indicative of a mistrust of the Deputy Head's motives for the change. Sometimes, this mistrust is actually well placed.

We have all been guilty of reading about a new initiative or a piece of research that seems so conclusive that it is bound to lead the way to positive change. There is nothing wrong with drawing enthusiasm from such experiences but be wary of being driven by your enthusiasm. Check that the most pressing student needs in your school (ideally, these will be what drove the design of your School Development Plan), are being addressed with the change you instinctively want to make. If you are sure of this, communicate it to others as part of your implementation plan. Not only will this enable others to trust your motives, but it will also set a standard that all change should be a response to student need. This is a powerful reminder to others who will also have their own change initiatives in mind. If student need truly drives change, and everyone starts from a shared understanding of what the most pressing student needs are, there should be synergy and mutual benefit to all changes taking place.

Be evidence informed

Having made sure that you are being driven by student need, you must then ensure that this standard continues to be maintained through each phase of implementation. When you are explaining a change you want people to make, be clear about the evidence base for what you are asking them to do. Although no evidence can be 100% reliable, the growing accessibility to a rich bank of educational research available to school leaders means that we can ensure that changes we want to make are driven by what would appear to be 'best bets' – those actions which are most likely to have a positive impact on student learning. Linking your requests to the evidence base will strengthen the trust others have in your motives and in the efficacy of what you are suggesting. It will also send a clear message that what is important is improving standards because you have invested time and energy in finding out the best ways to do just that. You haven't followed a fad or adopted what the school down the road has told you has worked, you are being driven by what the evidence indicates as the way forward. The inherent message is that you expect others to do the same. This is important because improving schools has to be about the students, not about the status or praise that comes the leader's way as a result. This is precisely the kind of thing that erodes trust because others will see that kind of leader as one who needs to have the limelight, needs to appear all knowing and needs to be beyond the support of other 'non-leaders'. That kind of leader also ignores the support that is available to them which in turn means that students miss out on the considerable breadth of expertise that could otherwise enhance their experience.

Leverage support

Drawing on expertise, both internal and external is a vital aspect of building trust and setting standards. You are embracing the vulnerability that comes with saying, *'I might need some expertise on this one and I think this person has it, so they can support me to support the students.'* This builds trust from others, and it also ensures that you are confident in using expertise to improve standards. Once again, we see that the same action can address both sides of the paradox of setting standards rigorously and maintaining trust supportively.

Sam Gibbs is the Trust Lead for Curriculum and Development at The Greater Manchester Education Trust. Sam shares how she worked alongside a Deputy Head of a school within her trust to help improve the school standards and build supportive relationships.

PROFESSIONAL PERSPECTIVE

By Sam Gibbs – Author and Trust Lead for Curriculum and Development at The Greater Manchester Education Trust

Key to my role in leading curriculum and teacher development across our Trust is working closely with the Deputy Heads in each of our schools. This poses challenges, but also significant opportunities.

The Trust system is still relatively young in the sector and for some more experienced Deputies, they may have spent most of their time in role self-directing, with high levels of autonomy. Leaders who work in a family of schools often have the benefit of additional expertise they can leverage from across the Trust, from colleagues within the central team with a particular remit, or from leaders in the other schools. If they are able to harness this expertise effectively, it can bring support, capacity and fresh thinking. Of crucial importance is developing relationships between colleagues built on trust and psychological safety.

Working together on complex problems necessitates honest reflection and a lack of ego. For Deputies to really benefit from the expertise of others, they need to be willing to 'lift up the bonnet', which can feel very exposing. But recognising areas where deep, domain-specific expertise is needed, and then being open to receiving it, is so important. It has personal benefits – it can increase knowledge and performance in specific areas of work, and enhance credibility to staff. More importantly, it models the value of collaboration and continuous professional learning. Leadership is not a solo sport – ultimately, everyone in schools and Trusts is working to the same aim, which is to better the lives of the children and communities we serve.

Strong working relationships with our Deputy Heads require mutual respect, compromise and vulnerability on both sides. Between us, we must manage the inevitable tension between the emerging priorities of a school within the Trust, and the needs of all schools within the organisation. Sometimes, this requires a Deputy to recognise that an approach which may serve them or their context is not in the best interests of the greater good – for example, a preference for a particular assessment strategy or exam board. It can be difficult to let go of preferred ways of working but where leaders embrace deep, purposeful collaboration, they see the benefits of collective wisdom and reduced workload through less duplication of effort.

Where Deputies have embraced collaborative working in our Trust, we have seen real improvement in the quality of education. Together, we developed a set of principles which we want to underpin design and delivery of the curriculum. Deputy Heads are the colleagues who lead this work in our schools – my role is to support them to do that work as effectively as possible. Recently, I worked with the Deputy for Curriculum at one of our schools, where he had identified variability in the quality of planning and delivery. We explored the issues together through discussion with staff, looking at planning documents and undertaking quality improvement activity. Analysing the problem collaboratively, we recognised a lack of clarity about how to plan the curriculum around subject-specific concepts and big ideas.

Together, we:

- Co-created a series of CPD sessions for middle leaders, based on an evidence-informed framework for curriculum design.
- Planned a sequence of coaching questions for the Deputy Head to use when meeting with middle leaders, to support them to apply the framework.
- Met middle leaders together to identify any areas for further support, and planned additional CPD sessions responsively.
- Provided leaders and teachers with curriculum handbooks, to ensure easy access to the latest evidence and research in curriculum design.
- Continually reviewed the emerging work together, and refined our approach where needed.

One outcome of our work was revisions made to the Trust Great Teaching Charter, which reflects our mutual learning. The benefits of working closely with our Deputies are always reciprocal – I have learnt a great deal from them to enhance the work I do across our schools.

4

Leading whole school areas

Introduction – delegation vs control

When people feel that their thoughts are welcomed, valued and respected, they grow and they develop within their roles. Former US Navy captain, David Marquet transformed his submarine's leadership from command and control to delegation with remarkable results. Faced with a crew trained to follow orders but possessing superior technical knowledge, Marquet realised traditional approaches would fail. (Marquet, 2013)

Captain Marquet vowed not to give orders for a raft of tasks and decisions. Instead, he delegated decision making to his team within a framework focused on intent. Team members present situations and explain their proposed actions and intended outcomes. Marquet's role was to check that the action was safe and appropriate for the mission. By prioritising those two factors (competence and clarity) he successfully delegated control. Subsequent inspections achieved the highest grades in US submarine inspection history. Marquet had created an environment for thinking, giving his team psychological ownership of their decisions while valuing their contributions.

Schools, like submarines, are too large an organisation for one person to make every decision. Marquet's experience offers a valuable lesson for Deputy Headteachers leading a whole range of whole school areas, and that is that of delegation: meaningful delegation increases both organisational effectiveness and personal growth. This chapter explores a collection of whole school leadership areas and the ongoing paradox of retaining decision-making consistency while empowering others to take the lead and drive your vision.

But why is this desirable? Firstly, you reduce decision making delay. If a middle leader must wait for your approval before implementing decisions, delays multiply across the organisation. Secondly, one of your roles as a senior leader is to develop people. Development requires people to think, and they need to know that their thoughts are valid and welcomed. They need opportunities to try things that they haven't done before and your delegation gives them the opportunity to do that.

Let's consider two key caveats; delegating 'the stuff you just don't like doing' to others is not what we are talking about here. For the middle leaders to grow, delegated responsibilities must matter and challenge their existing skill set and understanding. Captain Marquet, despite vowing never to give orders, retained sole responsibility for giving the most serious of orders – the orders that led directly to combat. He did this because he felt it was his 'moral and ethical responsibility', unwilling to burden others with such accountability (Marquet, 2013).

As Deputy Head teacher, you must retain overall authority for certain, such as recommending that a teacher is placed on a support plan or conducting parent meetings to write a risk assessment for their child. It simply wouldn't be the decent thing to allow others to carry that responsibility just to avoid being held accountable.

PERSONAL REFLECTION

What tasks or decisions do you feel would be unfair to delegate within the role of Deputy Headteacher?

_____
_____
_____
_____
_____

Considerations for delegation – collaboration

Sims (2017) found an opportunity for collaboration was one of the factors which had the greatest positive impact on teacher job satisfaction. It is fairly obvious that people are, on the whole, likely to value the chance to contribute to the decision making that impacts their working environment. What is less obvious is that people are often quite happy to assume the responsibility that comes with this important role in the decision making and this is a key ingredient of what healthy collaboration really is. It is linked, inextricably, to positive accountability (see Chapter 7). For now, it is enough to understand that collaboration doesn't just mean everyone firing their suggestions at the leader who then has to find a way of tweaking the intended decision to incorporate all of the suggestions. This would likely lead to a kind of lethal mutation of the original idea that would weaken its impact. It is a case of everyone understanding that if they offer a suggestion about how a particular idea should be implemented in their department or Key stage, they are accountable for its success.

Accountability does not mean that they will be hauled in front of the Deputy Head to be reprimanded if something goes wrong but it does mean that they are responsible for justifying their intent and that it is the right thing to do. Just as Captain David Marquet's navy team were. Indeed, Gwyn Ap Harri was clear in Chapter 1 that trust is not about blind hope but includes that 'show me' moment. This, in many ways, achieves the same aim as interrogating the intent.

One way of scaffolding this kind of thinking is to provide the key guiding principles, the aspects of the whole school area that must be present in any form of implementation and allow those you are delegating to use this as a framework for thinking about their ideas and whether they can justify the connection to the key ingredients. This is a theme that we will continually refer back to in each of the whole school leadership areas we explore below.

Considerations for delegation – culture

Another way to ensure that everyone is working under the same core set of principles in their decision making is to pay careful, strategic and deliberate attention to the culture you are trying to create around the leadership of your whole school area.

Hall (1976) established the analogy of culture being like an iceberg. What you can observe above the surface is the visible culture and this is generally quite easy to change. It is things like the dress code or the provision of wellbeing days. These are important and they are perhaps easily understood as being about the climate of the school – what you can see and observe and how it makes people feel. Hall proposed that this makes up about ten per cent of overall organisational culture and that the remaining 90 per cent exists subtly below the surface, out of concrete sight but certainly more influential in the destiny of the organisation. These factors are to do with beliefs, values, communication styles and attitudes. The key understanding for the Deputy Headteacher is that everything you do sends a signal indicating what is important in the organisation, especially what is important in the area of school life that you lead. Consider the Deputy Head who gives very public orders and instructions – what message is that sending about the value they place on empowering others to make decisions? Or the Deputy Head who walks past litter on the floor but then urges others to take care of the environment. What message does this send about collaboration and hierarchy?

So, what should we signal as important? Kraft and Papay (2014) identified six factors that separate schools where staff plateau and schools where they keep getting better over sustained periods. Culture was one of these factors and they identified that, within that, mutual trust, respect, openness and a commitment to student achievement were the most positively influential.

Considerations for delegation – coaching and mentoring

We have already noted the importance of delegation for growth and there is further evidence for the efficacy of this. Deans for Impact (2016) produced five principles of effective deliberate practice and this presents a useful way of viewing delegation. For clarity, the principles were:

- Push beyond your own comfort zone
- Work towards well-defined specific goals
- Focus on practice activities

- Receive and respond to feedback
- Develop a mental model of expertise.

As previously stated, it is important that you retain decision making for any aspects of the whole school area that you lead that are single points of failure. It would be irresponsible not to do so. What we mean by this is that any mistakes that others make, while problematic, are unlikely to be fatal. Delegation of such decisions are growth opportunities for the person you are delegating to and growing towards expertise is a long-term process that requires deliberate practice. As such, we can view the things that you choose to delegate to specific individuals as opportunities for a kind of deliberate leadership practice. How you choose to support the individual will depend on their level of existing expertise and knowledge.

If the appointed delegate possesses the necessary knowledge to make good decisions and is clearly aligned with your key ingredients, then coaching may be the type of support you offer. You guide their leadership thinking through questioning and reflection exercises designed to enable them to gradually build up and critique the solution to the challenge of implementation. With their existing mental models of middle leadership, you provide the scaffold for them to check their decisions against the principles and key ingredients you have set. However, for some people, leading is a whole new challenge. Think here of a new Head of Department. Without the existing mental models of leadership that come with experience and deep subject expertise, they are likely to need more guidance in their decision making. As such, mentoring them by helping to fill gaps in their knowledge and sharing insights that they may not have yet is the way to go. Sometimes this can mean offering suggestions; other times it means directing their attention to the details that they should base their decision on.

Another area we explore as we move through the remainder of this chapter is:

When to coach – allowing the teacher to make the decisions for themselves. When to mentor – offering suggestions and knowledge that the mentee may be missing.

PERSONAL REFLECTION

How have you seen (or would you like to see) the five factors Deans for Impact (2016) noted exemplified in school leadership?

_____
_____
_____
_____
_____

Push the circle of influence

Overall, leading whole school areas requires delegation. It requires delegation that is skilfully timed and given with clarity. You have to be sure that when delegating to (usually middle leaders) you have clearly considered three things:

- The principles and key ingredients of your leadership area that you won't compromise on
- To what extent you have signalled mutual trust, openness, commitment to student achievement and respect in how you have delegated

- What kind of individual support you will offer – when to coach and when to mentor. And, crucially, when to do neither and allow the individual to go forth and lead on your behalf.

These considerations are born from an understanding of the dynamics of leading whole school areas, or indeed any areas which are too large for one person to retain control of and can be understood using Figure 8.

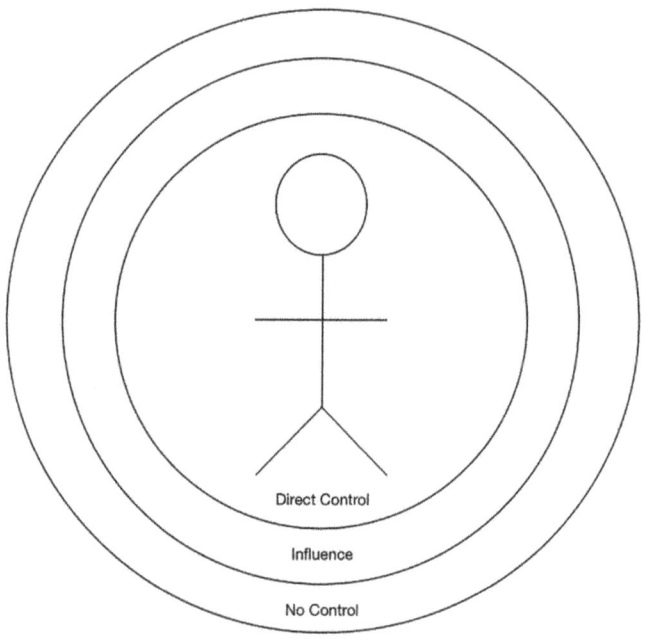

FIGURE 8: *Circles of influence, adapted from Covery (1989)*

In Figure 8, the person in the middle is the Deputy Headteacher; the inner circles are the things within your direct control. For example, the key ingredients or the design of the implementation strategy. The second circle is the things that you can influence. For example, the extent to which those you are delegating to work and behave in a way that is aligned with how you want them to work and behave. The third circle represents the things you cannot control. For example, a teacher in their first year of teaching who has encountered a challenging class. That doesn't mean that you can't help to resolve that situation but the existence of it in the first place is beyond your direct influence. Skilful, meaningful delegation will enable you to push the boundaries of your second circle – the circle of influence increasingly wider as you enable others to take on responsibility that will help them to grow, aligned with your values and ways of working.

Leading the curriculum

> 'Curriculum is the entire lived experience of the child' (Waters, 2022, p.26).

This reminds us of the scale of leading the curriculum. It reminds us that the curriculum is more than what takes place in individual lessons. It is the web of connections that we build for pupils over their time in our school and how we ensure that these are increasingly relevant and meaningful. It is every trip and experience we give, every piece of homework we set and every enrichment activity we carefully select. And, for the leader of whole school curriculum, this exists across a range of subjects, the majority of which they might have little or no expertise in.

So, how can an effective curriculum leader harness the powers of collaboration, delegation and mentoring and coaching, all around an established set of key ingredients to ensure effective curriculum leadership?

Control and influence

Let's begin by reflecting on Figure 8. With the Deputy Headteacher for curriculum in the circle of control, the circle of influence will most likely be middle leaders – Head of Departments or subject leads. The circle of no control is then populated by the teachers within those departments. And so, the circle of control first. What are the key ingredients of curriculum leadership that should be set by you as the Deputy Head in charge of this area? Professor Dan Willingham wrote that 'memory is the residue of thought' (Willingham, 2009). This reminds us of the link between memory and learning and is a useful place to start when coming up with your key ingredients, your principles of curriculum that you want to ensure that all middle leaders understand and remember when making decisions.

Key ingredients

David Ausubel (2000) proposed the idea of meaningful knowledge. According to his theory, key, generalised knowledge sits above specific detail of what is taught. The idea is that we decide on the most meaningful general concepts, and then select the detail of each unit of work in order to build an increasingly sophisticated understanding of the generalised knowledge (Ausubel, 2000). This understanding of overall curriculum design principles is echoed by Andrew Percival in his chapter for *The researchEd Guide to Curriculum* (2000). He explains the idea of selecting the key concepts to be continually revisited throughout a student's school trajectory and explains that the concept should be developed and explored with deeper sophistication each time it is revisited. (Percival, 2020).

Trust, respect, openness and commitment

The Deputy Headteacher cannot specify the key concepts for each and every subject to be built around. This would be too great an undertaking for one person and send a powerful signal that they did not trust the expertise of the Heads of Department. But what they can do is ensure that every Head of Department understands the idea of building a curriculum around key concepts. You set the principle of curriculum design around key concepts and then you hand the autonomy for designing the concepts for their subject over to them.

The key here is to remember to do this through trust, openness, respect and a commitment to student achievement. Consider approach A and B below and the clear differences between them.

Approach A

'I can't do the next bit so I'm going to need you to each do it for your subject by this deadline'.

Approach B

'I don't have the expertise that you have within each of your subjects so it is only right that you have the autonomy on exactly what these key concepts should be. Hopefully, you are as excited by this collective project as I am and can see how building curricula in this way is going to make it easier for students to remember the key information. I understand that you might be concerned about the time this could take. So, my ideal deadline would be… Do you think that's realistic or do we need to revise it?'

Approach B places value on the contributions of the Heads of Department or subject leaders. It also represents genuine empowerment. You have delegated meaningfully. The experts are better placed than you to decide what the key concepts in each subject should be so this is the right call in terms of prioritising student achievement. Because it shifts responsibility into the hands of the experts, it presents a genuine opportunity for growth. Captain Marquet explained this as 'moving the autonomy to where the information is' (Marquet, 2013).

Coaching and mentoring

Having understood the key ingredients and empowered others with the autonomy to make decisions for their subjects, how do you provide coaching and mentoring support to ensure that those you have delegated to feel trusted and competent? Let's consider what their roles may actually be. You want to push your influence as wide as you possibly can and so it is crucial that the Heads of Department ask their teachers to engage in tasks will embed your key ingredients. You want them to:

- Work with their department teams to come up with the key concepts for their subject
- Quality assure those concepts
- Work as a team to come up with the detail that will exemplify those concepts
- Quality assure so that the key concepts are becoming increasingly challenging as your students progress through the curriculum.

Leadership expertise of any kind does not always correlate to experience. However, those Heads of Department who have more experience are likely to bring more of their own beliefs to the decisions that they make. The support you give them is probably more appropriate if it uses their existing beliefs as a start point and then gradually seeks to align these with the key ingredients of curriculum design that represent your key principles. This is where coaching can come in.

CASE STUDY: GEMMA

Gemma has been leading science for five years and is a well-respected member of staff. She has great subject expertise and her team are always happy to follow her lead because it inevitably leads to at least partial success. They are a little subservient to her, and over the last five years, there have been staff who have moved on because they feel there is a lack of value placed on their thinking and involvement. Nonetheless, the department is one of the top performing departments in the school.

Coach: OK, so let's start by checking in on our collective aim. From the sessions we did looking at curriculum design, what is the key goal of the work you are doing as Department Head?

Gemma: Well, I know what the key concepts of the curriculum are and so my goal is to get the rest of the science team to help design the content of each unit of work.

Coach: Do you feel you will get maximum commitment from your team by giving them the key concepts?

Gemma: Are you saying I should let them decide? They don't have enough experience to know more than I do!

Coach: I'm suggesting that you may achieve more buy-in if they have co-constructed the concepts with you. Could you guide their thinking so that they arrive at the conclusions that you want them to?

Gemma: I suppose I could give them a set of ten and ask them which seven they think we should use?

Coach: What other options do you have?

Gemma: Well I could let them suggest all the different ideas they have at the start but then I'm worried that the meeting will run away from me if their ideas aren't quite right or if they misunderstand. I guess I could mitigate that by making sure I was really clear in my explanation of what a key concept is and perhaps give some examples?

Coach: That sounds like two options in one! That's great – any more?

Gemma: I could give them some pre-reading to do about concepts and then complete a Google form with which ones they think are really important and why. Then I could use this as the start point of the meeting and could pick out the ones where more than one person has suggested it, especially if those are ones that I really think are important? That would also mean I would have time to plan how to respond if their understanding seems to differ from mine.

Coach: That's really clearly thought out. Which option do you think you want to go for?

Gemma: I'll go for the last one because it means I have the time to assess their understanding and then plan how to respond to it with how I lead the meeting.

Coach: And on a scale of one to ten how likely do you feel right now that that will be successful.

Gemma: If I'm honest, I'm still unsure because it's not how I would have instinctively done it so probably a six out of ten but I am definitely up for giving it a try.

Through coaching, Gemma has been able to apply her expertise and align this with the Deputy Head's core principles of ensuring that mutual respect and collaboration sit at the heart of curriculum design.

By contrast, a less experienced middle leader may not have such a clearly defined mental model of their own expertise or of the task at hand. This is where mentoring may be a more appropriate approach to take.

CASE STUDY: ALFIE

Alfie is an inexperienced Head of Department who has been in the role for only three months. He was identified as an excellent practitioner and his enthusiasm and dedicated work ethic have meant that he has been given the opportunity to lead the department. He has no previous middle leadership experience and so this represents a brand-new career stage for him.

Mentor: OK, Alfie, so I want to start by going through the key principles of curriculum design and how you might apply those with your team. Does that sound like it could be useful?

Alfie: Definitely. I'm really not sure that I have the leadership experience to get people to buy into this idea.

Mentor: OK, not to worry. Experience has to build and that's as much about making mistakes as it is anything else. So, tell me what your ideal concepts for history would be.

Alfie: Chronology, power, change and consequence, similarity and difference.

> **Mentor:** OK, they sound good. It is likely that some people in your team will have different ideas to you and others will have the same ideas, so it's going to be important that you present your ideas, value theirs and buy yourself time to consider your decisions in light of their ideas.
>
> **Alfie:** How would I do that?
>
> **Mentor:** Well, you have a couple of options. You could go to the meeting with your team and offer your ideas as a starting point and then let them offer theirs. If you get any ideas from them that you don't think are appropriate, then you could say that you'll do some thinking with their ideas in combination with your own and come back to them with a proposal for how you move forward. Or, you could send out a Google form in advance of the meeting to collect their ideas first and then prepare your response that you then give at the meeting itself. I suggest that you try option 2 first because then it will give you more time to prepare for the meeting and what you are likely to discuss there.
>
> **Alfie:** OK, so I'll send round a form asking for what they think the key concepts are. I could start the meeting with any of the ones that I definitely think are good ones and then spend some time discussing some of the others once I've had a chance to think about how I might explain them?
>
> **Mentor:** Exactly. If you want to come back to me when you've received their responses, feel free.

Through both approaches, the Deputy Head in charge of curriculum has embedded the principles of curriculum leadership into the practice of their direct layer of influence. They have pushed the boundaries of their circle of influence closer towards the circle of no control. The middle leaders are more firmly aligned with the Deputy Head now and are more likely to lead in a way that reflects the underpinning principles that the Deputy Head values. The next task for the Heads of Department will be to quality assure the detail chosen to exemplify the key concepts and the resources produced in relation to these. In both cases, the task of the Deputy Head is to maintain influence over the core principles and ingredients and try to ensure that trust, openness and a commitment to student achievement permeate the exchanges between Heads of Department and their teams. To do this effectively, the Deputy Head should continue to weigh up the benefits of both coaching and mentoring approaches.

PERSONAL REFLECTION

What are the differences between coaching and mentoring approaches?

_____
_____
_____
_____

In what scenarios would you use each approach?

_____
_____
_____
_____
_____

Andrew Percival is Deputy Headteacher at Stanley Road school in Oldham. He is also the author of the influential blog *Confessions of a Curriculum Lead* and has written about curriculum design for researchED. He has consulted for an Ofsted working party on curriculum and is a regular contributor to educational discourse on X using the handle: @primarypercival. Here, Andrew shares his insights about curriculum design and how he ensured that subject leaders had ownership and autonomy while working with the key ingredients that he set out.

PROFESSIONAL PERSPECTIVE

By Andrew Percival – author, keynote speaker and Deputy Headteacher of Stanley Road Primary School, Oldham.

As we began our work on developing the curriculum at Stanley Road Primary School, we initially defined five principles that would form the framework for thinking about the substantial task ahead of us. The five principles were:

- Acquisition of knowledge is at the heart of the curriculum – focusing our time on learning domain-specific knowledge is the route to improving pupil achievement in each subject.
- Knowledge is specified in fine detail – it is only possible to build pupils' understanding of challenging curricular concepts through the accumulation of small units of knowledge – these need to be set out very clearly so that nothing is left to chance.
- Knowledge is acquired in long-term memory – a curriculum should be constructed and taught in a way that secures the content so that it can be easily recalled in the future.

LEADING WHOLE SCHOOL AREAS

- Knowledge is carefully sequenced over time – careful thought should be given to the optimal sequence in which to teach the content of the curriculum. As a result, pupils are more likely to understand and remember what they have studied.
- Knowledge is organised into subject disciplines and is derived from discourse within the subject community – each subject should have a distinct pathway within which knowledge is built systematically over time. The way we select the knowledge to be learned is informed by subject experts.

With a shared understanding of this framework, as curriculum leader, I was then able to work with individual subject leaders to clarify how this would apply within the context of each subject. Although I had a clear vision of the overall aims of the curriculum, I was acutely aware that I did not have the subject-specific knowledge that was needed to interpret this for each of the subjects.

Through a sequence of collaborative meetings, we began to define some of the key concepts that we intended to develop through the curriculum. We then also began to map out a tentative overview of the sequence of learning. Subject leaders were given time out of class to research and write a unit plan for an agreed topic (e.g. Year 3's block of work on rivers in geography.) This unit consisted of a series of 'knowledge statements' that specified the precise content that we wanted pupils to acquire as a result of studying this topic. After this unit had been written, I then met with each subject leader to discuss the content they had planned, how this would connect with other units of work and to allow them to explain how this aligned with our shared principles for curriculum development.

Where staff had demonstrated that they were confident with the task ahead, they were then given

> greater autonomy, along with allocated time, to write other units in the curriculum. Where staff were still finding their feet, we arranged to meet again to review progress. Through collaboration and delegation within a clearly defined framework, we were not only able to construct a more coherent curriculum for our pupils but also empowered our subject leaders to take ownership of their curriculum and develop further within their roles.

Tips for success

Some other top tips that are useful in the leadership of curriculum:

- Use curriculum development timelines. These track what you have done over a set period of time in curriculum or subject leadership. They specify when actions were taken, what the actions were and the purpose of the action. They can also be used as a planning tool for future intentions but can be used as part of new staff induction or to support conversations with inspectors and other outside agencies.

- Create structured opportunities for teachers to give feedback to Heads of Department about what is and isn't working in practice in terms of the curriculum. Encourage the department head to feed this back to you so that you are aware of where the tensions and key decisions are at any given time. It is then up to you to decide whether a coaching or mentoring approach will best support the Head of Department in their decision making.

LEADING WHOLE SCHOOL AREAS

- As part of any planning process, encourage the use of a pre-mortem: a process in which the team project ahead and imagine that things have gone wrong. They then identify what the most likely cause of this would have been and plan actions to prevent the failure from transpiring. This is a really useful tool for developing a sense of shared, healthy accountability and allows the team to claim ownership of the issue and the solution.

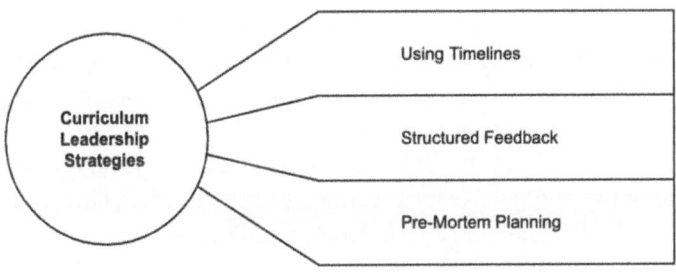

FIGURE 9: *Enhancing leadership and collaboration*

Leading behaviour

Everyone wants students to behave in school. Everyone wants behaviour to be at a standard that allows teachers to get on with teaching without having to compromise their lesson. Everyone also wants students to behave in line with the values that we think will serve them well when they venture into the world as adults. Why then, is this subject, with such widespread agreement on the ultimate destination, so divisive in terms of the processes that school leaders use to reach the destination?

Debates around mobile phone bans, the efficacy of detentions, accepting or not accepting bad language from students, have exemplified the binary nature of how the behaviour issue is seen in schools.

In a world where we are constantly searching for universal truths, beliefs that we can apply to any situation with the required surface features, debating behaviour approaches very often divides more than it unites. This is because the notably intangible and difficult to define aspects of culture, context and values play such a crucial and formative role in each of our opinions about behaviour. It taps into something very personal about each of us and so when we read or hear a view that contradicts our own, it often cuts across our ethos, our core reasons for being in education in the first place. But it needn't be so. An acceptance of the idea that a 'good' approach to behaviour is driven by values, culture and context, is to accept that there can be no single universally applicable approach. And, while this is frustrating, it also liberates us from feeling like we are either in the right camp or the wrong one. Culture, context and values must drive your leadership of behaviour as a Deputy Headteacher.

Context is king

The leadership of behaviour is first about understanding where you are leading. There is little value in ploughing time and energy into a weekly celebration of the school's values if the classrooms are in constant chaos due to bad behaviour. Context is the key here and an understanding of the challenges faced within your context is crucial to your successful leadership of this whole school area.

If your school's major behaviour issue is low level disruption, for example, regular calling out in response to questions asked by teachers, then that will require a different response to if there is widespread dangerous behaviour, for example, students throwing chairs in response to being given a detention. If there is a culture of carelessness and a lack of pride in the school environment from students, then the response should be different to if the major issue is a lack of positive relationships between staff and students. Your context can also be influenced by the physical setting. For example, former Headteacher of Burlington Danes Academy, Dame Sally Coates wrote: 'I'm... intrigued by schools where students march in line, sometimes even reading books in silence – a model borrowed from a chain of charter schools in America... but our long corridors, large student body and sprawling site aren't conducive to silent transitions, so we settle for an insistence on calm, quick transition, supervised by SLT and teachers, who we ask to meet and greet their students in the corridor outside their room' (Coates, 2012).

Your first priority should be to establish a clear understanding of your context, both through your own experience and by consulting others. In order to do this, you need to speak to people. Surveys and interviews with class teachers, support staff, students and parents will all help to build up a picture of exactly what the unique challenges are for your setting. If staff are telling you that they feel unsafe, that will alert you to a different kind of action than if they say they feel frustrated at widespread apathy towards learning. Pay close attention to the views of students and parents who might offer very different views to that of staff but whose views are no less insightful. Once you have collected these views, you will have a good idea of what the most challenging aspect of behaviour is in your school and when paired with a consideration of the key physical context of the building, you are likely to have a framework for informed decision making.

You must also understand who is in your circle of influence. Who is it that you have direct influence over in terms of how they address behaviour in school? Whether this is Heads of Year, a pastoral team or Heads of House, these are the people who will either reinforce or undermine the system that you put in place around behaviour.

> **PERSONAL REFLECTION**
>
> In your school, if you had overall responsibility for leading behaviour, which roles would inhabit your circle of influence?
>
> _____
> _____
> _____
> _____
> _____

Once you understand your context, informed by the viewpoints of others, and you have identified the members of your circle of influence, you must then consider how you begin to influence them. Essentially, you want people to act in a way that aligns with the spirit of your behaviour policy. The challenge is that you can't detail every single potential scenario and how to respond to it in your policy – it would be unusable. Instead, you have to align key people – those in your influence circle – with a common set of values that will guide their decision making in terms of behaviour.

Values guide behaviour and that is what makes them so key.

Leading personal development

Anna Woodcock is a Deputy Head at Greswold Primary School in Solihull and one of her roles has always been centred around personal development. In her personal perspective she talks about her experience of managing this role.

PROFESSIONAL PERSPECTIVE

By Anna Woodcock – Deputy Headteacher at Greswold Primary School, Solihull

Leading personal development effectively can be challenging. The modern-day pressures of teaching may lead to PSHE lessons and other aspects of personal development being 'squeezed' in favour of core curriculum subjects. Personal development, in itself, is complex and multi-faceted with some components related to specific curriculum areas; others that are gained through school life. How do you tackle mobile technology/media which they access at home and the potential exposure to dangerous people and situations that this carries? For 15 years, I was Personal and Social Development Lead and when I explained the different elements of my role colleagues often asked, 'Well, isn't that basically everything?' Sometimes, it did feel that way and the same can be said of leading personal development. It can, at times, feel daunting.

But, for all its challenges, having a leadership role with a focus on personal development and inclusion is immensely rewarding. Seeing staff engaged in deep philosophical debates with children, the care and respect with which they treat each other and watching pupils grow and flourish as individuals is truly a privilege. So how do you approach this role?

Everything that we do at Greswold is underpinned by our values of BRICKS (Belonging, Respect, Independence, Curiosity, Kindness and Success). These provide a framework to all that we do, including personal development. They are the building blocks which create a secure foundation for our curriculum (including behaviour) and pupils are given many different opportunities to explore these in different contexts. In addition to this, as leaders, we ensure that BRICKS are woven into our strategic approaches, for example our 5-year plan, SIP and Pupil Premium Plan. Similarly, SMSC is interwoven into all aspects of learning. This approach enriches our curriculum and ensures that development of children as individuals is at the heart of our strategic planning.

From a personal perspective, I've found being organised with a set of clear systems in place to be able to triangulate your approach is important. Part of this is ensuring you have mechanisms in place to ensure you understand how the different components are taught: curriculum, collective worship or other means. Another key part is enabling *all* staff (not just teachers) to recognise the importance of personal development as well as understanding that it needs to be intentionally taught, rather than just caught. It takes a team approach as inconsistency can easily undermine an otherwise effective programme. Pupils are very perceptive as to who is just 'talking the talk'. As adults, we know that our emotional state has a huge impact on our ability to work effectively as well as our relationships with others. If we want our pupils to achieve their potential, they need to feel happy, secure and that they belong.

Each school is unique and there isn't a one-size-fits-all approach to effective personal development. However, in my experience, a key to success is embedding your core values in your school community whilst building, establishing and nurturing relationships between leaders, staff, pupils and families. Ultimately, pupils need to feel that their voices are heard and that they really do matter.

Anna makes some crucial points about the leadership of her whole school area and they are all applicable across a range of areas. For example, the fact that often, the true value and impact of your leadership in one area is that it begins to bleed into other facets of the school. Your presence is often felt more widely, the better the job that you do and the more able you are at generating interest and enthusiasm among colleagues. Anna also provides a practical tip of first understanding and then planning and organising how different components of the school system are taught. Despite this being something that is seemingly simple, it is rarely ever easy and so we are reminded of the importance of ensuring that we do the simple things well, for it is those things that lay the foundations for everything else that follows.

The value set

> 'Teaching is not just about imparting knowledge; it's about shaping character and instilling values' (Strickland, 2023, p.43).

Sam Strickland, a leading voice in behaviour management conversations in schools, offers a reminder of how values work. They underpin everything we say and do and so create a kind of decision-making code that everyone implicitly (in time) understands. Once a core set of values have been understood and accepted by enough people, they will become just part of what people in your organisation do. Collective commitment is powerful so it is vital that when you choose your values, you choose them well, with the context of your school in mind and in consultation with parents, students and staff.

> ### PERSONAL REFLECTION
>
> What core values would you apply to behaviour in your school?
>
> _____
> _____
> _____
> _____
> _____

When establishing your school's values, you should also have input from all stakeholders, including, perhaps most crucially, the Headteacher. But then, how do you ensure day-to-day engagement with those values from those who matter most – those in your circle of influence?

The key here is communication and messaging. You need to communicate the values both explicitly and implicitly and you need to create activities that will facilitate your circle of influence doing the same. Let's assume that your circle of influence includes Heads of Year. You might choose to meet with them and ask them to name behaviours that align with each of the school's values. For example, what behaviours reflect a commitment to 'high expectations'? You could then co-construct your behaviour policy around these. Allowing your Heads of Year to have that level of input and responsibility will increase the likelihood that they take that message out into the school and promote it through their words and actions.

Another explicit strategy that you could use is assemblies. Making use of assemblies to talk about the behaviour you value and the behaviour that you don't, or perhaps better still, allowing your circle of influence to do this, will gradually sow the seeds of expectations. If this message is delivered by Heads of Year, you will also begin to push that circle of influence a little wider as your message, in its original form, moves closer to the teachers on the ground.

Values in action

There are other things you can do to embed the kind of behaviours that exemplify your values. Katherine Berbalsingh is Headteacher of Michaela Community school in Wembley. On their website you can read about how highly they say they value discipline. You can also read about their 'strict' uniform policy. Clearly, discipline in action on a daily basis. They also talk about the importance of students being 'compassionate, considerate and kind'. At lunch time, students sit in round tables of 8 and are expected to serve each other – again, values played out in expected behaviours. Whether or not you agree with the policies and approach of Michaela community school is beside the point. They present an example of identifying values and then building activities into the day that put those values into practice. And remember context is king. In another geographical or physical context, these values may not be the ones that school leaders choose to overtly promote.

Being kind and compassionate are certainly worthwhile but it may be that another school feels that their context enjoys this as 'standard' and choose to put their focus on other values instead. As such, these activities and policies may not be appropriate in another context, and that is fine too. Context drives values and values drive behaviour.

As Deputy Headteacher in charge of behaviour, it is your job to guide the collaborative design of the values and to build policies and actions into the school day that make it easy and rewarding to act in accordance with those values.

> **PERSONAL REFLECTION**
>
> What activities would you include in the school day to make sure your values are reflected in what everyone does?
>
> _____
> _____
> _____
> _____
> _____

The culture conundrum

You will likely have an ideal vision for the actions that reflect the values you want in your school. However, designing these activities – like students serving each other at lunch time, or the uniform policy – should not fall to one person alone. If you want these actions to be valued by all, you need the help of your circle of influence. By bringing them into a collaborative process of designing the activities that will support each of the values, you allow them to feel that they matter. And they do. They are, after all, the ones with the most day-to-day experience of the activities that you want to put in place. They are also the ones who are the first port of call for students when something does go wrong. So, asking for their contribution to the design of activities will, result in a better set of activities than you would have designed on your own. It also gives ownership to the people closest to the activities, moving the decision closer to where the information is.

When you have a group of people who are genuinely invested in the success of a behaviour approach, others begin to follow. They begin to see 'the way we do things here' as being reflected by the activities that you and your team have designed and when this happens, it spreads like wildfire.

Management expert, Peter Drucker famously said: 'culture eats strategy for breakfast' (Drucker, 1991). Ultimately, you can have the very best behaviour policy in the world and a set of activities that are fully connected to the organisation's values, but if you can't embed those into the culture of the school's behaviour approach, you will be forever frustrated that the impact of your strategy and ideas goes no further than your (very limited) circle of control. People need to be on board with the ideas that you propose because the successful implementation of these ideas depends on their commitment to them. If they understand the rationale behind the strategy, they are far more likely to get behind the idea.

The key ingredients

Overall, for your leadership of behaviour to be successful, you should remember the following key points:

- Ensure that you fully understand the context of your school – physical, geographical and historical and ensure that you seek out the views of others to cross-reference with your own experience.

- Create a set of values that the whole school has had input into.

- Work closely with your circle of influence to agree activities and actions that you can embed into the daily life of the school that will exemplify your shared values.

- Support your circle of influence to keep the messages front and centre for all staff through assemblies and modelling the values at every opportunity.

- Remember that you need alignment to create a culture so don't rush to implementation before you have collective agreement because culture eats strategy for breakfast!

At this point, cast your mind back to the start of this chapter and to the story of Captain Marquet. While he empowered others to make their decisions, he also kept some decisions back, only for himself. One of these decisions was when to fire a missile.

PERSONAL REFLECTION

What are the decisions that only you can make as Deputy Head?

_____
_____
_____
_____
_____

This chapter has explored the central theme of how to balance controlling a whole school area of leadership at the same time as empowering others to lead these areas 'on the ground'. To bridge this paradox, we suggest that Deputy Headteachers use meaningful and skilful delegation. Encouraging others to take on the shared responsibility for the success of an initiative not only empowers their decision making authority and

LEADING WHOLE SCHOOL AREAS

allows them to grow but it also allows them to demonstrate vulnerability. That is why the support we promote, in the form of coaching and mentoring is so important.

True shared understanding and healthy shared accountability comes from collaboration. Value the views of those 'close to the information', as Captain Marquet says. Think carefully about how collaboration is designed to facilitate the type of thinking that you value in your whole school leadership. We highlight the importance of pushing the boundaries of your circle of influence. Middle leaders often drive your leadership and collaboration. Value, empowerment and opportunities for growth will go a long way towards motivating them to lead your vision. One potential barrier you might encounter is time. What should you do if your circle of influence likes your ideas but pushes back due to a perceived lack of time?

Consider this quadrant:

High workload – High impact	Low workload – High impact
Low workload – Low impact	High workload – Low impact

If you experience concerns from colleagues about time constraints, ask yourself (and them) where on the quadrant the initiative falls. If you can agree that it is in quadrant one, it is likely that something else should be removed to make space for the new idea given that it is collectively agreed that the impact will be high. If it sits in quadrant two, it should be straightforward to explain why the time investment is worthwhile. Any initiative that lands in quadrant three should probably be reviewed to increase the potential impact before bringing it back to colleagues, and any initiative that sits in quadrant four should simply be avoided.

In addition to curriculum and behaviour, assessment, inclusion, SEND and pastoral are all common whole school areas that Deputy Headteachers might lead.

PERSONAL REFLECTION

What key takeaways from this chapter could you apply to any area of whole school leadership?

_____
_____
_____
_____
_____

What are your pivotal decisions?

To close this chapter, we return to Captain Marquet's analogy. Marquet suggested that certain decisions carrying the most serious consequences, rested solely with him because he felt the moral and ethical responsibility should be his and no-one else's. To delegate responsibility for this would not have been the decent thing to do and would have burdened team members with a decision and consequences that they did not deserve to have to deal with.

So, in the context of the leadership of whole school areas, what are the leadership decisions that you feel should sit with you for moral and ethical reasons?

PART 2

Cultivating personal and professional growth

5

Developing support staff

The backbone of the team

Schools cannot function without support staff. The premises manager who quietly makes sure that the boilers are serviced on time, the PAT testing is up to date and the legionella tests have all been carried out, removes worries that leadership teams didn't even realise were there. The front office team represent the school responsibly in every parental interaction, knowing that the impression they give reflects the collective organisational ethos. These people create the sense of coherence that reassures external stakeholders that there is a clearly defined and purposeful way of working. From teaching Assistants, whose role is perhaps the most varied of any in school, to counsellors and whole class teachers, ready to step in at a moment's notice to save the Deputy Head grappling with the impossible task of covering absent teachers and not spending an entire year's supply budget before October half term. They truly are essential in the school delivering on its pledge to provide first class education.

As close to the 'ground' as one could ever be, support staff also feel the day-to-day challenges and impact of under-developed implementation as much as any other group. One common challenge is how to protect support staff morale. Consider the difference in the platform afforded to support staff in comparison to teaching staff. Often, there are no weekly briefings, line management meetings often go no further than sharing planning for upcoming lessons and, in some schools, the appraisal process for support staff is little more than a nod to the paperwork police with no genuine attempt to allow people to articulate their hopes and aims for the future.

And now acknowledge the contrast in the value placed on development for support staff compared with teaching staff and leaders. Where is their allocated training time necessary for developing their practice? Perhaps they attend courses but where is the mechanism for them to roll this training out amongst their colleagues? For now, assume that the lack of value placed on their training opportunities contributes to low morale. Take a moment to consider the other contributory factors to low support staff morale. We will revisit this idea later in the chapter.

PERSONAL REFLECTION

What factors can you think of that affect support staff morale?

_____
_____
_____
_____

And, how can these factors positively or negatively affect morale?

_____
_____
_____
_____
_____

Managing and developing support staff illuminates another key challenge in the life of a Deputy Headteacher. How do you manage these important individuals in a way that maximises efficiency and support for other teachers and leaders and simultaneously invests time in developing support staff? The best development – the kind that all staff are entitled to – is ongoing. We don't mean a day out of school for a training course. Instead, we mean regular development of their practice with feedback and reflection playing a crucial role. There are no hard and fast answers to the paradoxes facing Deputy Heads but there is a framework for thinking about the challenges you face that is likely to help you consider key elements alongside the unique context of your school. In the remainder of this chapter, we will consider how to truly understand support staff perspectives, the importance of maintaining positivity, engaging with development and aligning support staff development with whole-school PD.

Through considering each of these factors, we hope to provide a framework for understanding the context of support staff development. This will then help you to make decisions that will keep them feeling valued and developed while also maximising their impact on students in your school.

Understanding support staff: listening to and hearing their voices

If you want to understand support staff, you must create opportunities for them to contribute to the most valuable discussions in school and you must work alongside them to remove the barriers that they feel and perceive in their role. This is not just about making people feel valued (although of course, this is hugely important) but it is about gaining their insight to ensure that every person in the organisation remains fully aligned with decision making. Too often, the first time a member of support staff finds out about a whole school classroom change is at the same time as the children. Consider how teachers would feel if the first time they found out about a new classroom environment audit checklist was when the Deputy Head walked in to administer the audit. The likelihood is that even if the audit was an excellent piece of work, the teacher would still feel negatively about it because they had not been consulted. That is often the reality for support staff.

Research has shown the importance of involving all stakeholders in the decision-making process. Emira's findings note that 'leadership, among other things, should focus on creating an atmosphere conducive to fostering collaboration and participation in decision making.' (Emira et al., 2013). This is not to say that support staff, (or teachers) should have a vote on any changes within school but their opinions should be valued and considered.

One common rebuttal to the suggestion that support staff should have a voice in the decision-making process is that their contracts usually preclude them from being in school outside of the hours that the children are in school and therefore, not available when these conversations take place. Although this does present a challenge, it is far from insurmountable and requires strategic communication to be a core leadership priority. To exemplify this, let's look at how you can communicate change with the school effectively.

> **PERSONAL REFLECTION**
>
> Consider the support staff who are in school outside of the hours that students attend – this might include office staff – for example. What barriers limit them accessing high quality PD?
>
> _____
> _____
> _____
> _____
> _____

Change through the support staff lens

John Kotter's *Leading Change* (1996) is a seminal work on how organisations can lead change effectively. The successful Deputy Head might benefit from the model that Kotter presents and apply Kotter's lessons at every opportunity. One such application opportunity is the creation of the School Development Plan (SDP). Some leaders choose to complete their SDP on their own, others with just their SLT present. We propose that all staff are involved in this process. Firstly, this creates a sense of equal value. But it also provides a valuable reference point for decisions that are made throughout the year. By constructing the SDP process with Kotter's model of change in mind, you can ensure that subsequent changes that take place throughout the year make sense in that they link closely to those earlier agreed upon broad aims. Read the table below and take a moment to complete the personal reflection that follows.

Kotter's change stage	SDP activity	Impact on support staff
Create a sense of urgency (give people a reason or purpose to pursue change).	Provide pivotal evidence to support the establishment of a broad aim for the school that is then refined through the contributions of all.	Understand the direction of the school as a whole.
Build a guiding coalition (encourage commitment from your group).	For each broad aim, have a group of people who will be responsible for maintaining the focus of the people in their team on the aim.	Support staff have representation in the guiding coalition and as such leadership from within rather than above.
Form a strategic vision (evaluate the past and look towards future goals).	Identify broad changes that everyone wants to see and agree timescales for re-evaluating progress.	Allows support staff to view all changes with the context of the longer-term plan. They know how many changes we are aiming for as a school this year and so change fatigue is less likely to occur.
Enlist a volunteer army (get people together who have similar aspirations and are looking to achieve the same common goal).	Allocate people who have a particular motivation to be more closely involved on the operational aspect of a change.	By having Support staff representation, there is a vested interest in collective support from all support staff. Again, the leadership comes from within rather than above.

DEVELOPING SUPPORT STAFF

Kotter's change stage	SDP activity	Impact on support staff
Remove barriers (pinpoint what is stopping the school from making progress in specific areas).	Identify barriers to success and allocate actions to be taken to people in order to remove them.	Allows a voice for support staff to identify barriers but also ownership and involvement in the removal of them which creates another layer of vested interest in the success of the change.
Generate short term wins.	Be granular with your success criteria so that success is experienced early on.	Support staff will have mini check in points to work towards at which they will celebrate the success of everyone's contribution to that point.
Sustain acceleration.	Acknowledge that to achieve some broad aims, more than one change will be needed and some changes will be unknown at this stage.	When initially unknown changes are made later in the year, this will not feel like a deviation of direction for support staff as they will be able to view the changes in the context of the broad aims.

Kotter's change stage	SDP activity	Impact on support staff
Institute change.	Make every action clearly linked to the broad aims of the organisation.	This will allow support staff to see the relevance of all actions which makes their actions feel purposeful. With purpose comes improved morale because they can see how their individual contribution improves what the whole organisation is able to offer.

The above proposal for how to co-construct the SDP with the full involvement of support staff is built on two principles:

- keep people connected to purpose
- communicate the relevance of actions.

In the first section of this chapter, we acknowledged the unhappy trend for support staff morale to seemingly be lower than that of other people in the school. From communicating why an action has relevance, we get purpose and motivation and, from purpose and motivation comes improved morale. So, it's worth it… but once you start you have to stay committed to these two principles.

What makes the SDP process successful is that it provides time to think and space to explain. These are essential for support staff to not just contribute to the development of the school but also understand why it is developing in the way that it is. There needs to be regular communication opportunities throughout the year which continually relate back to that first SDP planning session. For example, consider the same change implemented in two very different ways as described below:

Context: The Deputy Headteacher has worked with the Head of the English department monitoring whole school reading approaches. They have noted that excellent progress has been made since the start of the year and this is due, in some part, to the work of support staff helping the least fluent readers make accelerated progress in this area. The two senior leaders decide that they would like the support staff to do the same work but with a set of students whose reading fluency is in line with age related expectations to see if they can make the same amount of progress as the least fluent reading group did.

Scenario A

Context: A bi-weekly meeting of support staff, led by the support staff member who was part of the guiding coalition for developing reading across the school.

'You'll remember that during the SDP planning day, we all agreed that this year we wanted to improve the reading fluency of pupils across the school. We seem to have made quite a bit of progress in this area judging by the English lead's most recent monitoring and so they have asked that we try to move things forward further by repeating the work we did with the least fluent readers with the other students in the school.

We really need to discuss three things:

- Do we feel we have the capacity to fit more of this reading fluency work in at the moment?
- If not, could we stop doing something else that is not having as much impact to make space for more reading fluency work (which clearly is having a huge impact).

- What other considerations do we need to make before we make this change?

I have invited the Deputy Head to join the end of our meeting, so that we can feedback our thoughts on these three areas. I will then meet with him to make an implementation plan if we all agree that this is something that will benefit the pupils.'

Scenario B

Context: A weekly email about the following week's calendar and events which is sent out at 3.00 pm on a Friday afternoon.

'Dear colleagues,
Following the huge success of the reading fluency interventions this term, we will roll this out across a second group of pupils in Key stage 3. The pupils have been chosen and the timetable for each member of support staff has been amended accordingly. Your timetables will be sent to you at some point over this weekend. Please don't feel you need to look at them right away! Monday morning will be absolutely fine. Well done again on all the impact this work has had so far. Looking forward to seeing how much impact you can continue to make next term!'

Clearly, there are several issues with scenario B and this is also an exaggerated situation. However, it is not that far removed from (I am slightly embarrassed to say) emails that I have sent to support staff earlier in my leadership career. So, when viewing the two scenarios side by side like this and seeing how much better scenario A feels, why do we find ourselves often reverting to something closer to Scenario B? We feel that there are three, frankly quite uncomfortable realities that feed into this.

Lack of time: it is quicker for the Deputy Head to send the email in Scenario B and monitor to make sure that the requested action is taking place. But this approach will likely lead to a sense that support staff have been excluded from a wider conversation about whole school progress. So, although there was initial time saving, the hidden cost lies in the decreased effectiveness of the intervention.

Perceived lack of skill to engage in reflective practice on the part of support staff: uncomfortable yes, but in many cases, true. There is a hugely misplaced assumption that support staff do not have the same level of reflective skill to be able to engage thoughtfully with the questions posed in Scenario A. This is simply not the case and needs to be regularly challenged whenever the suggestion of simplifying communication to support staff is made.

The assumption that support staff are just not that invested: Herzberg (1968) showed that job satisfaction was linked to purpose and meaning and there is no reason to think that this does not apply to school support staff. They care about being part of something bigger than their own individual efforts just as much as every teacher and leader in a school does and they should be communicated with this in mind.

PERSONAL REFLECTION

How frequent do you think support staff communication needs to be in your setting? How could you ensure that it links back to that initial SDP session to keep the framing of changes relevant?

_____
_____
_____
_____
_____

Communication through leadership from within

Having established that support staff involvement in SDP planning is the desirable model to pursue, who should actually facilitate it? Let's go back to Kotter's model of change. He promotes the establishment of a guiding coalition. Support staff should be part of the guiding coalition for every change so that there is representation of varied perspectives, but this also has the effect of creating a leadership role from within. By allowing the conversation from Scenario A above to be led by the support staff member who is part of that particular guiding coalition is one way of clearly demonstrating that you believe support staff are capable and that you value their input. It is also likely to elicit more honest and reflective responses from support staff as a result. Bear in mind though that this is not the same thing as appointing a chief member of support staff. There are instances in which this kind of role is useful but what we are advocating here is the ability of any member of support staff to ask for membership to a coalition linked to a change that they have particular interest and/or expertise in. This should not be limited to those members of support staff deemed 'best' and will only serve to create another layer to the hierarchy at the expense of the leadership from within that we noted earlier in this chapter.

Naturally, there is some communication that should come from the leadership team directly. For example, (with specific reference to teaching assistants), Skipp and Hopwood (2019) found that:

'Respondents from participating schools reported that TAs were being deployed to support teaching and learning in three broad ways:

1. whole-class support
2. targeted in-class learning support
3. targeted intervention delivery.'

(Skip and Hopwood, 2019)

The reality is that as the student body and whole school priorities change within a school, so do the roles of support staff. For example, a school who predominantly deploy their support staff for targeted in-class learning support and then find that their low prior attaining group of pupils are not making as much progress as their peers, may feel the need to rapidly change how support staff are deployed and deliver more targeted intervention. While this change should be related back to those broad aims agreed upon in the SDP planning session, the communication of this kind of change is more appropriately delivered by a member of SLT.

Understanding perspective

One final word on support staff and the importance of understanding their viewpoint as well as creating a culture that facilitates open conversation. In my own school, I have had members of support staff tell me that they don't feel I spend enough time in their part of the school. While this was a difficult message to hear, it was their valid perception and the start of an important conversation. We discussed the competing demands of my role and my commitment to ensuring that everyone in the school feels valued. Upon reflection, I had assumed that because the support staff in my school are very high performing and very experienced, that this in itself would make them feel valued because of the important contribution they were making to the students. The outcome of the open culture we have and the conversation that flowed as a result was that I committed to spending time every week in their part of the school and they agreed to taper their expectations of the amount of time I had to offer to that commitment. Everyone listened and left happy (including us).

Engaging with development

While the precise reasons for support staff having less engagement with PD in schools than teachers are up for debate, the reality that provision for them in this area is lacking in comparison to their teaching colleagues is difficult to dispute. Fortunately, the same principles for helping teachers to engage in PD apply to support staff, but when planning to engage people with these principles we must understand the context of their start point. For many support staff, this start point often includes a belief that PD is not really for them or that it is a tick box exercise to show that they are 'getting something'.

So, how do we suggest that Deputy Heads responsible for developing support staff engage them with development? All of the suggestions below are supported by Bridget Clay's (2017) article, 'CPD for school support staff' which is an excellent article and well worth reading to supplement the thinking that follows.

As you read through the following suggestions, keep in mind this quote from Professor Rob Coe:

'Great leaders find ways to implement PD to maximise its impact, to prioritise long-term benefits over shiny quick fixes, and to make time for PD by reducing the time teachers spend on less effective things.' (Coe, 2023).

Professor Coe's thoughts remind us that providing high quality PD comes with a time cost, but the bold Deputy

Headteacher will back themselves to make this time count so well that the value added to practice will outweigh the initial investment of time. If we are to bridge the paradox of maximising resource deployment during the school day and providing support staff with the time to think and develop, we must back ourselves to make the development time count and be bold in our allocation of that time.

> **PERSONAL REFLECTION**
>
> Consider your school's current timetabling arrangements and support staff deployment as well as their working hours. How could you logistically offer a form of ongoing development to each role?
>
> _____
> _____
> _____
> _____

Linking to whole school professional development priorities

If we are one school and all pushing in the same direction, then we should all be contributing to the same priorities. Anything else suggests a different level of value being applied to one group of people than the other.

At Birkbeck Primary school in 2022, reading was identified as a whole school priority. Teachers received several training sessions on different aspects of the teaching of reading and support staff also had one hour per week where they all worked collaboratively on developing their roles to teach reading. As one important part of their role was to read 1:1 with children: they received training on reading fluency, understanding what it is, the different aspects of it and how to develop each one both individually and simultaneously. As Deputy Headteacher, Adam was proud to hear support staff explaining how they were developing prosody, automaticity and accuracy to visitors at the school and the end of Key Stage 2 outcomes also improved significantly since this commitment to developing support staff practice in this area started. While this is certainly not the only measure to judge impact by, it is a useful indicator.

Whatever your whole school priorities are (and remember, set those as part of your SDP planning day with the involvement of support staff), make sure that you consider how support staff will develop their practice to contribute to these aims in the same way as teachers.

PERSONAL REFLECTION

How could you facilitate a contribution from support staff around the school development plan and how could you incorporate their personal professional development into it?

Keep it regular

> A poem is learned by heart and then not again repeated. We will suppose that after a half year it has been forgotten: no effort of recollection is able to call it back again into consciousness.
>
> (Ebbinghaus, 1885)

When building PD cycles consider how memory and attention work. Hermann Ebbinghaus's work on memory and forgetting is useful here. Ebbinghaus (1885) proposed that as soon as something has been taught, we begin to forget it. As the quotation above shows, without interrupting that forgetting process, we will reach a point whereby recollection is just too difficult to be done successfully. There is little to be gained in terms of long-term impact for support staff practice from a one-off training session on just about anything. Instead, you must plan to revisit learning at regular intervals, spaced deliberately closer together at the start of a process and then further apart as distance from initial learning increases. In much the same way as your pupil's revisit topics throughout the year and revise for their final exams, your staff should regularly revisit their PD targets in order to reach new milestones in their career development and whole school progression. Revisiting in this manner will help to keep new learning in the consciousness of support staff until it is embedded in long term memory well enough to be recalled when they want it with automaticity. Only at this point have we achieved lasting impact on practice.

Provide time to share and collaborate

While it is difficult to get all pupil facing support staff together at the same time regularly, it is a challenge worth doing everything possible to meet. Enabling support staff to share and collaborate on how they have applied professional learning is essential in creating a sense of collective endeavour and purpose that makes people feel part of something greater than just their own work. The motivational effects of this should not be underestimated. And, returning to Professor Rob Coe (2023), this time must be given during the school day. Send the message that you are so confident in the impact of the PD that you are providing and in the ability of your support staff team that the time you set aside is a worthwhile investment. Yes, there will be things that support staff are not able to do as a result of investing contracted time in their development but, in the words of Professor Coe: 'schools can't just add PD on as an extra thing; something must be taken away. Fortunately, most schools should be able to find plenty of time-consuming things that add less value than professional learning' (Coe, 2023).

Use student needs as a source of evidence when selecting PD opportunities

Because 'support staff who work with children, just like teachers, should engage in identifying student needs and directing their learning accordingly' (Clay, 2017).

PD for support staff should be driven by pupils' needs within the school context. This highlights the need to involve support staff in the construction of the SDP. Part of this process identifies the whole school priorities and designs actions to address them. PD is then the mechanism for improving the effectiveness of the actions.

Support professional learning with a focus on it during appraisal

If we want people to take PD seriously, we have to value it. This value comes back to appraisal. By taking the time to identify how each individual can enhance their own learning to contribute to the wider school priorities, we show support staff that we take their learning seriously and that their learning is a worthwhile investment for the school to make. We believe that they will have an even greater impact on the students as a result. It's hugely empowering for people in any organisation to feel that by developing a particular area of their practice, the people running the organisation believe they have the potential to positively impact key outcomes. Of course, the key to effective appraisal conversations is to make the link between the school priorities and the learning of the individual and to co-construct targets accordingly.

I have worked in schools where every support staff team member has the same targets. While the reasoning is that their roles are all similar and are all contributing to whole school priorities in the same way, this neglects the fact that they have unique challenges in the contexts in which they work and all bring differing levels of expertise relating to whole school priorities. Co-constructing individual targets gives you the flexibility to take each person's existing expertise and individual context into account when shaping targets which all contribute to the overall school priority.

I was recently thrilled to hear the incoming Headteacher at my current school introduce herself to staff with the line: 'I am coming in with an approach to listen and understand'. As with all aspects of leadership, the successful Deputy Head must begin developing their team of support staff by listening and understanding. Only once you have gained real understanding of the context can you hope to provide PD that will gain the investment of effort and belief from the recipients.

The paradox of this chapter was how Deputy Heads can maximise resource deployment *and* provide the conditions for effective PD – most notably time during the school day. Time spent on PD is time away from the students. But we propose that the bridge to this paradox is in the quality of the PD provided. If it is truly impactful then the time investment will be reimbursed with improved provision for pupils in the long term. So, how do we ensure that it is impactful? There are many context-driven considerations to take and we have summarised these below.

Key takeaways

- Establish the relevance of support staff PD by involving them in the construction of whole school priorities. This will likely reduce resistance because the 'point' of the subsequent PD will be more relevant.

- Keep the PD regular so that the key messages remain front and centre as people embed the new learning.

- Provide PD during contracted hours. There is simply no better way of showing how much you believe in the value of development for your support staff and this provides them with vital time to think.

- Ensure collaboration takes place – this will add to the sense of being part of something greater than themselves.

- Ensure professional learning is consistently linked to whole school priorities and driven by individual development need during the appraisal process.

Before we move on from the development of support staff, we have an insightful professional perspective. Attiye Passey is an Assistant Headteacher at a First School in South Staffordshire and she is also an Evidence Lead in Education (ELE) with Staffordshire Research Schools. Attiye provides her thoughts on the importance of support staff in the classroom.

PROFESSIONAL PERSPECTIVE

By Attiye Passey – Assistant Headteacher at a First School in South Staffordshire

Building positive relationships with support staff in schools is one of the most important investments we can make in creating a strong and consistent learning environment for children. When we become overwhelmed with other school responsibilities, it's easy to forget that support staff are not our personal assistants; they are highly skilled practitioners who, when supported in the right way, can transform the classroom experience.

The strength of this relationship is not built solely on the shared responsibility for the children. Relationships deepen when we take the time to know each other on a personal level; finding out about their weekend, sharing a laugh or treating each other to a coffee. Genuine care builds mutual trust and respect. Our roles bring daily challenges and can sometimes feel lonely. Having strong, supportive relationship provides an anchor on tougher days, making challenges feel more manageable. You may even discover that your colleague has hidden skill sets that would benefit future learning opportunities. Midway through a clay-modelling sessions with my Year 1 class, I found out that my TA had a degree in Art and specialised in clay! I called upon her experience immediately and guess what? She loved it. Empowering all staff to speak up, take action and recognise their strengths drives school improvement and brings staff together.

An equally important step is ensuring that you and your support staff share the same vision. Taking the time to talk through classroom values, expectations and aspirations for the children fosters consistency. When everyone works towards the same clear goals, it reduces confusion and increases opportunities for success.

Coming from an Early Years Foundation Stage (EYFS) teaching background, I have seen how powerful this collaboration can be. In classrooms where outstanding practice is observed, it is often difficult to distinguish who is the teacher and who is the member of support staff. Both move seamlessly together, giving silent signals and adjusting to meet children's needs in real time. To me, the ultimate superpower is looking around a room full of engaged young learners, engrossed in their play, while adults work purposefully to celebrate and extend that learning. We should all aim for harmonious classrooms and not ones made of a hierarchy of staff. Such harmony, I believe, is only possible when relationships are built on mutual respect, shared vision and genuine care.

6

Developing teachers

The core business of any school is teaching and learning. Whatever other distractions, responsibilities and preoccupations you are faced with, improving the quality of teaching should remain front and centre of your leadership mindset and practice.

Systematically developing teachers and your school's approach to teaching has both an impact on the leadership of teaching and learning and also on how people are led in your school and on the prevailing culture of the organisation. This is captured in Figure 10 below, adapted from Van de Brande and Zucollo (2021). Their model proposes that providing regular and effective PD, will not only improve teaching quality, and therefore student outcomes, but teachers will be more motivated and less likely to leave the profession suggesting that a healthier organisational culture is a potentially powerful secondary impact.

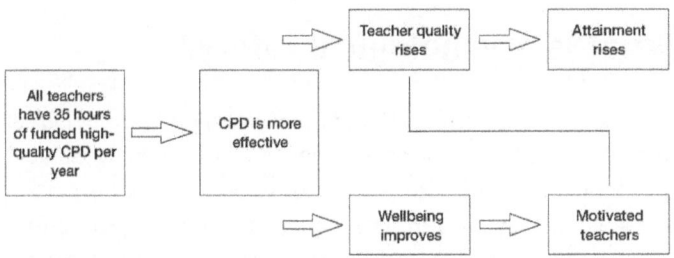

FIGURE 10: *Systematic development of teachers, adapted from Van de Brande and Zucollo (2021)*

More on the ingredients of effective PD later but first, a delicate question of implementation that requires careful consideration. How do you successfully bridge the paradox between being relentless in your drive to continually improve teaching while also building and sustaining a supportive culture for teachers? With so many teachers leaving the profession citing the pressures of the job and excessive scrutiny of their practice, it is vital that the drive for improvement comes intrinsically from the teachers themselves as a result of the culture you create around PD.

Positive, well-designed PD is likely to improve the quality of teaching and lead to a culture of development, sustained improvement and crucially, psychological safety – the feeling of being able to take risks and make mistakes without fear of negative consequences.

The remainder of this chapter will focus on the design and tools likely to have a positive impact on the development of teachers but will also explore the implementation strategies and contextual considerations which are likely to have a positive impact on school culture. But first, let's look at the concept of psychological safety and why it is so important in the context of teacher development.

What is psychological safety?

Clinical psychologist Carl Rogers first described psychological safety in 1954 as the conditions in which employees feel 'unconditional worth' (Rogers, 1954) valued for their expertise even when they make mistakes. Most people would prefer to work in an environment in which mistakes are accepted as part of the learning and improving process but from a leadership perspective, there is enormous organisational value in establishing psychological safety.

DEVELOPING TEACHERS

In 1999, Dr. Amy Edmondson studied clinical teams and the mistakes that they made in the context of a hospital and found that teams who had more good outcomes also made more mistakes than those who had fewer good outcomes. Upon further interrogation, she found that in fact, the teams with less good outcomes were actually making as many mistakes as those with the better outcomes but were hiding theirs. In contrast, the teams with better outcomes had the confidence to be honest about the mistakes they were making. A culture in which mistakes are embraced, free of judgement, is a factor in organisational effectiveness. So why can't schools work in the same way?

For leaders, psychological safety isn't a vague aspiration – it's observable in daily behaviour. Can staff admit mistakes without fear? Ask for help? Push back or challenge ideas respectfully? These are the real barometers of a safe team.

Take a moment to reflect honestly on your team dynamics. For each statement, rate how true it feels in your current team (1 = Not at all true; 5 = Very true).

Statement	1	2	3	4	5
1. Team members admit mistakes openly without fear of embarrassment or punishment.					
2. People feel comfortable asking for help when they're struggling.					
3. Team members can challenge each other's thinking respectfully.					
4. It's safe to take risks or try new approaches in our team.					

Statement	1	2	3	4	5
5. I regularly model vulnerability by admitting when I've got something wrong.					
6. We regularly debrief after initiatives to discuss what went wrong and why.					
7. Everyone's voice is heard in discussions, not just the loudest or most senior.					
8. Mistakes are treated as learning opportunities, not sources of blame.					

Reflection prompts:

- Where are we strongest as a team?
- Which area most needs improvement?
- What one thing can I do differently this term to improve psychological safety?

PERSONAL REFLECTION

Think of a time when you owned up to a mistake. How was this received?

_____
_____
_____
_____
_____

> What does this tell you about how psychologically safe your workplace is?
>
> _____
> _____
> _____
> _____
> _____

CASE STUDY: LYN

The job of the Deputy Head responsible for teacher development is to normalise mistakes. If individuals feel safe enough to admit to their personal mistakes and weaknesses, this will often reveal patterns and commonalities to you as the leader. This may lead you to consider that the 'mistakes' are actually products of poorly designed initiatives rather than individual errors.

In the late 2000s, I was a young and inexperienced teacher and I remember being told to implement a new strategy for questioning that involved me pulling lolly sticks out of a cup, each with a child's name on them. The child whose lolly stick was pulled out was then the one who had to answer the question. The strategy wasn't particularly well explained and certainly wasn't supported by any research or real world evidence. I tried dutifully for months to implement the new strategy but was met with sustained failure.

Eventually, I plucked up the courage to speak to a more experienced colleague (Lyn) and to admit my failings to

> her. I was stunned to find that she too could not seem to get the prescribed strategy to work! Imagine our shock when we began talking to other teachers in the school, only to find that every person was hitting a pedagogical brick wall. Soon after, Lyn, (our elected representative) took our concerns to the Deputy Head at the time. They addressed the issue and the problem was solved. If we had only all felt the psychological safety to flag our concerns in that first training session, we would have saved months of anxious worrying. More importantly, our students would have benefited from so many more lessons that were delivered better.

The leader who thinks they need to have all the answers

The case study shows how damaging it can be when teachers feel like their mistakes are failures. The tennis player, Billie-Jean King once said, 'losses aren't failures, they're research' (King, n.d.) and nothing could be truer in the world of education. Psychological safety is characterised by teachers discussing mistakes and things that just don't seem to be working. It is teachers and leaders working together to try to find a solution, not the leader imposing an answer on the struggling teacher. The impact of the leader who says: 'I'm not sure how to solve that one but I have a hunch that X may work' cannot be underestimated. Even if you are certain of a solution, if you are in the stages of trying to establish psychological safety, frame your response as a hypothesis.

We will discuss formal observation later on but for now, let's assume that the vast majority of teachers find it anxiety inducing. This is due to the judgemental nature of observations, which arises due to the hugely unbalanced power dynamic at play. For a start, an observation is usually part of an organisational routine, which immediately divorces the process from the aim of being about the individual. In the classroom, the observer is the perceived expert who views every action the teacher takes during the lesson through a critical lens of: 'I would have done it this way...' which then means the lesson becomes a bizarre attempt by the teacher to give the observer precisely what they want to see rather than what the students actually need.

What if that observation opportunity arose organically as a result of a teacher asking the PD lead if they had potential solutions for a problem they were experiencing? In that situation, consider the following response:

- *'I'm not sure how to solve that but 'X' may work. It has worked for me before in a similar context. Would it help if I show you what I mean?'*
- The teacher then observes the leader putting their idea into practice.
- They then meet to discuss the specific contextual challenges of the class that the teacher wants to overcome with a new strategy.
- This is followed by rehearsal, a period of a week or so to practise and then the teacher lets the lead know when they are ready for them to watch the new strategy in action.

We suggest that this process is far more likely to have a positive impact on practice because of the inbuilt psychological safety. Firstly, there is no 'correct answer' given by the leader when the initial question is asked. This breaks the expert-novice dynamic. Secondly, the leader is observed first. This makes it clear that observation is a research tool rather than a judgemental one because there would be no plausible use for a teacher judging the quality of teaching of the lead for teacher development. Thirdly, a contextual conversation follows. This makes it clear to the teacher that since context is the crucial factor in strategy selection, they are the expert because they have full contextual knowledge of their class. The period of practice enables the teacher to feel prepared and to focus on process over outcome which when the observation finally comes around enables them to concentrate on the part they can control – the process. Finally, by allowing the teacher to invite the leader to observe, they know what the observer is evaluating the effectiveness of. This removal of the unknown establishes a trust that underpins the psychological safety the teacher now has.

There's a challenge between ensuring psychological safety as described above and the responsibility that the Deputy Headteacher has to monitor/evaluate the quality of teaching taking place in classrooms. Remember that the role of the Deputy Headteacher is to *lead* these areas and not necessarily to do all the heavy lifting. The Deputy Head can have the responsibility of developing a coaching team whose job it is to develop classroom practice while also having the role of evaluating the quality of teaching in the school as a whole. What is likely to be ineffective is a situation where the same individual is responsible for evaluation and development at the 'ground level'. Another key factor here is to remember that the task of evaluating the quality of teaching in a school is more complex than evaluating the quality of each individual teacher. It is a case of looking for common practice across the school and this divorces evaluation of teaching quality from the quality of teaching of any individual teacher.

> **PERSONAL REFLECTION**
>
> What are the typical teaching and learning characteristics in your school? For example, what are the things that all or most teachers do really well? Are there any areas that all or most teachers need to develop, such as differentiation or start of lesson routines? To what extent does your current PD programme address these?

You are already enough

The above reflection creates a sense that improving teaching is a shared endeavour, that the role of the leader is to walk alongside the teacher. This goes hand in hand with the assumption that the teacher is already good enough and that the process is about their development, not continually proving that they are still meeting the base standard. This message will be more powerful if teacher development is completely divorced from judgement. So, if you are going to have formal observations, don't pretend they are about developing teachers, simply have them as part of the SLT's evaluative processes. If you can, remove data- or outcome-driven targets from performance management documents and replace them with (often less measurable) process-driven targets.

The DfE has announced an end to performance related pay, which we welcome as this was always another barrier to getting teachers to truly embrace their development areas.

Overall, establishing psychological safety is about teachers knowing that they are already good enough and that there are processes in school, of which they are actively in control that support their development. A small number of teachers don't always meet the standard that pupils deserve. This is a separate and more serious issue that is addressed in the section on accountability.

Work with principles

By distilling great teaching down to a set of clear, tangible principles, a Deputy Head in charge of developing teachers can establish the psychological safety that underpins sustainable improvement. Be careful not to fall into the trap of listing intangible fluff, however. Although 'excellence' is a principle, it doesn't give enough specific guidance on what teachers need to do to improve their approach. It is much more helpful to think about the broad components of successful teaching. For example:

- modelling and examples
- explanation and scaffolding
- checking for understanding.

This creates a mental model of what good teaching is and subsequently a framework for considering teaching in your school.

The foundation of this work is Barak Rosenshine's principles (Rosenshine and Stevens, 1986), later made more digestible in *Rosenshine's Principles in Action* (Sherrington, 2019). Thinking about teaching as a set of principles in this way gives teachers the licence to justify their own decisions which in turn gives them the confidence to make decisions. For example, a teacher who understands that they should be providing non-examples of new concepts is more likely to embrace developmental feedback on the specific non-example they chose to use in their lesson. There is a certain degree of safety to 'You applied the right idea (principle), but here is an idea for how you could have applied it more effectively'. Helpfully, this also provides a framework for improvement. The teacher is likely to understand why a given strategy is suggested to them if it fits clearly into the agreed principles of teaching in the school.

One crucial role of PD is to create alignment between teachers' mental models of what good teaching is – the framework of cues and related decisions that occur in the most effective classrooms. This is how you create consistency but it is also how you create psychological safety because teachers know that what they understand to be good teaching is shared by the leader.

PERSONAL REFLECTION

What do you believe are the most important principles of high-quality teaching?

_____
_____
_____
_____
_____

Understanding accountability

Accountability in schools means ensuring that everyone is doing their part to support pupil learning and wellbeing. There need to be systems in place to monitor, support and address performance at different intervals.

As a Deputy Head you are accountable to the Headteacher, governors, and to Ofsted. Within the school environment you are accountable to other teaching staff, the pupils, the parents. You need to hold others to high standards, model the standards yourself, support and facilitate improvements where possible and act decisively when standards are not met.

Accountability is often used as a threat to ensure compliance with instructions that have come from someone or a group of people in senior positions. For example, 'If you want to change the assessment system, that's fine but of course, you are accountable for the impact'. However, the evidence suggests that effective accountability *does* improve performance.

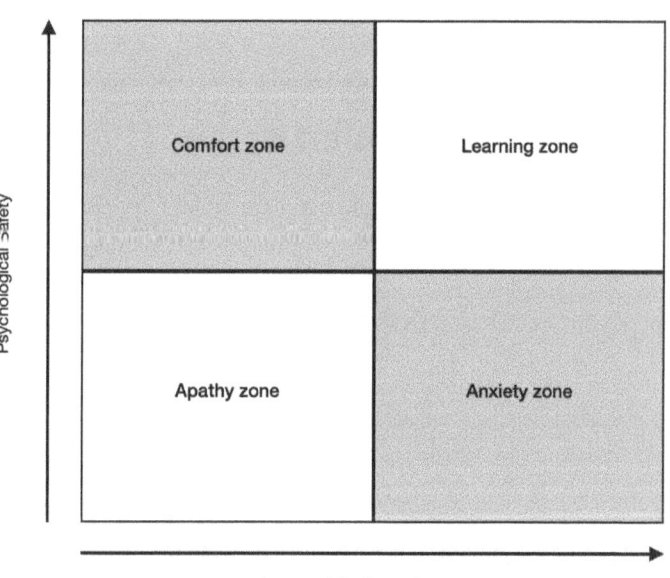

FIGURE 11: *Establishing psychological safety alongside accountability systems, adapted from Edmondson (2012, p.174)*

Figure 11, (adapted from Edmondson, 2012, p.174) shows the value of establishing psychological safety or an environment that encourages open dialogue and honesty alongside effective accountability systems.

High levels of psychological safety combined with low accountability places people in the comfort zone, a space from which development is at best laborious and at worst impossible. On the other extreme, low psychological safety and high accountability seemingly produces the worst of all environments with teachers in perpetual states of anxiety. And so, we return to the paradox: how do we create psychological safety and a culture of continuous improvement? Hopefully, you will now feel confident in your understanding of the importance of psychological safety and how you could begin to establish it within the context of teacher development. But it is also clear that a certain amount of 'push' must also be incorporated into our approach to developing teachers. People have to feel that they are being challenged without losing the support that comes from psychological safety. How exactly does a Deputy Headteacher bridge the paradox between being consistently challenging and unwaveringly supportive?

- Model vulnerability
- Reflect openly about things that haven't gone as planned
- Create safe spaces for dialogue
- Use anonymised surveys to encourage honest feedback
- Celebrate risk-taking by encouraging staff to share approaches that they have experimented with
- Act on feedback.

How was accountability originally intended?

Educational accountability goes as far back as 1976 when the Prime Minister James Callaghan identified a need to open schools up to people with a vested interest in their success, (Callaghan, 1976). The Education Reform Act, (1988) provided schools and school leaders with greater autonomy and accountability for the decisions they made. When autonomy and accountability are intelligently combined, student achievement increases (OECD, 2010). But, over time, the concept of accountability in the education sector has fallen victim to lethal mutation and become synonymous with monitoring actions and subsequent consequences.

Accountability in the context of a Deputy Headteacher's work describes a relationship between them and the teachers they are holding to account. The teacher has a responsibility to justify their *actions* or *performance*. If the Deputy Headteacher is holding the teacher to account, it follows that the teacher is providing the account (or explanation) for the actions they have taken and the outcomes of those actions. Crucially, the teacher should account for their actions in respect of all of the accountability relationships that they are a part of. Earley and Weindling (2004) identify four.

1. pupils (moral accountability)
2. colleagues (professional accountability)
3. employers (contractual accountability)
4. the market (market accountability).

There are two broad approaches to accountability: outcome-driven and process-driven. Far too much energy in schools can be spent on the accountability to those above teachers in the hierarchy and all too often, the accountability relationship is concerned with outcomes and results instead of processes and justifications for choices. Of course, this represents another paradox because often, results become the ultimate benchmark for the effectiveness of leadership. However, a results-driven approach ignores the fact that results are products of processes. Maintaining focus on the process will likely improve results too. A process-driven approach is characterised by teachers offering an account or justification for the choices they have made and working alongside the leader to unpick those decisions and choices with the aim of increasing effectiveness in the future. If this is truly the aim of accountability systems then we also create psychological safety because the conversation is not about condemning a decision that did not pan out as planned, or scapegoating the person who suggested the approach, but instead is about being accountable for the learning that comes from it. This provides fertile ground for further development and creates a self-improving model of accountability among your colleagues.

The challenge is finding the right balance between process- and outcome-driven accountability. While it's important to hold people accountable for results, sometimes if only one person is held accountable for both the process and the outcome, this can leave a person feeling isolated and defensive, as if they are waiting to be 'caught out' by a process.

There is a place for outcome-driven accountability, but how do we ensure that this is effective and does not undermine the self-improving effects of process-driven approaches? An outcome-driven approach to an accountability measure that sits with only one person suggests that it is that person who has full responsibility, not just for the outcomes but also for the processes. This creates a significant feeling of pressure and isolation and following that, defensiveness which in turn leads to many teachers feeling that the process aims to 'catch them out'.

To bridge the accountability challenge, Deputy Headteachers should foster psychological safety by walking *with* their staff throughout the process rather than dictating the direction. A powerful approach is to involve multiple people in the process, with each role contributing to a shared outcome. This distributes responsibility, which naturally leads to a shared accountability for outcomes. Trust between senior Leadership and teachers grows SLT members take ownership of processes and become accountable for the outcomes too. Consider the two contrasting examples below:

Happy Lane Primary school wants to set some really ambitious targets for their Year 6 cohort. They want 93 per cent of students to meet the Expected standard in Reading, Writing and Maths combined, to put them in the top one per cent of schools in the country. The class teacher, Olly, has been called to a meeting with the Deputy Headteacher to set a best case scenario target for the year group and agree on an action plan.

Scenario A

The meeting begins with the Deputy Headteacher telling Olly that last year the school got 95 per cent of pupils to the expected standard, and they expect the same this time around. They give Olly a list of actions to put in place, most of which are to do with after school booster sessions and prescriptive classroom approaches. The Deputy Head tells Olly that they will check on the progress that children are making every three weeks and that they expect to see improvement week on week as evidence of Olly's effectiveness at putting the Deputy Head's instructions into action.

Scenario B

The meeting begins with the Deputy Head presenting Olly with the end of year data for his class from the previous year. They then ask Olly to talk about any children who seem to have already been making excellent progress in the early weeks of the school year. They ask Olly to think about what he has done to help those children make the progress that they have.

This allows Olly to be accountable for success – an often-overlooked aspect of accountability.

The meeting then moves into a pre-mortem: Olly projects ahead to the end of the year and imagines a disappointing set of results (note that the Deputy Head does not put a figure on 'disappointing'.) Olly is asked to consider what is likely to have happened for this imagined scenario to occur. This gives Olly the opportunity to think about the potential barriers to the best-case scenario outcome.

This part of the process is important because, in contrast to scenario A, this approach acknowledges the reality that there are challenges that stand in the way of progress and that success is not inevitable so long as Olly follows a set of prescribed steps.

Once the barriers have been identified, the conversation moves to what needs to be done to remove those barriers if possible. This may include things like running extra booster classes or a 1:1 mentoring system for targeted pupils in the year group. Crucially, the Deputy Headteacher volunteers themselves to take on responsibility for delivering one of the actions. They also suggest other members of staff who could do the same.

This part of the process is important because it creates a sense of shared endeavour. Olly is not on his own. Others are contributing to the removal of barriers and so there is a shared accountability for the process being assigned, and, likewise, a shared accountability for the outcome.

The Deputy Head blocks out time in their calendar to deliver the actions they have taken responsibility for and then suggests a progress review date when all the actions identified can be reviewed alongside the most recent assessment data.

This final step shows Olly that the Deputy Head is taking their commitment seriously. They have blocked out the time in their own calendar which then makes Olly feel motivated to make sure that he too prioritises the actions that have been assigned to him. The suggested progress review date now becomes a meeting at which the effectiveness of all the identified actions will be discussed, once again reinforcing the sense that it does not all rest on one person's shoulders.

Clearly, scenario B is preferable. By taking on a small part of the accountability for the process and outcome, the Deputy Head has won Olly's trust and inspired his own commitment to the actions that he is going to be accountable for. This allows the Deputy Head to position themselves alongside Olly, yes, holding him to account for the implementation of agreed processes and subsequent results, but doing so with the added strength of their own example. Sharing accountability, even in small measures, creates a sense of shared endeavour that is then all the more likely to succeed.

Context drives professional development

Having considered the importance of psychological safety and the tricky balance of accountability, we now move on to the practicalities of how you can establish systems and processes that genuinely enhance teaching practice. 'Interventions work when they meet a perceived need in the school' (Sims et al., 2021, p. 55). All too often, leaders implement PD around an approach because they have heard that the approach has worked well in another school or because they have a personal interest in the intervention they want to implement. For example, they have read about retrieval practice and want to introduce quizzes at the start of every lesson. The evidence is clear though that impactful PD meets an identified need within the context of the school and that this should be the start point for planning and implementing change.

Early in my career, I worked with a Deputy Headteacher who was particularly taken by John Hattie's 2009 study, *Visible Learning*. In the study, Hattie's aim was to determine which common teaching practices had the greatest impact on student learning. He found that teacher quality and feedback were particularly influential factors and he calculated average effect sizes for each. The Deputy Head I worked with would conduct regular learning walks and would leave a sticky note on your desk with a list of strategies from Hattie's study along with their average effect size. For example, the note might say 'Activated prior knowledge – 0.93' implying that any activation of prior knowledge has an equal effect size of 0.93. Of course, this ignores the fact that within the averages of Hattie's study there was some excellent practice with effect sizes far exceeding 0.93, and equally some poorer practice with diminished or non-existent positive effect sizes. In short, it ignored the contextual application of activating prior knowledge.

Developing teachers by developing their instruction is undoubtedly the most logical approach but showing them a set of strategies and then asking them to 'do' those strategies in any form they possibly can, does nothing more than create a checklist. Too often that checklist is used to hold teachers to account over classroom processes in an approach divorced from context. I have seen schools that produce checklist feedback to teachers with each prescribed strategy evidenced in a 30-minute observation and those not seen automatically becoming 'next steps'. This can inadvertently limit teacher autonomy and creativity, and might even diminish their sense of psychological safety. Instead, encouraging reflective, context-sensitive support enables teachers to thrive, think strategically and engage in more meaningful PD.

Effective features of professional development programmes

Returning to Sims et al. (2022), context is king. An excellent Deputy Head will identify the needs that must be met by the PD programme in the school and will design it with the context of the school in mind. That said, while factors such as school size, staff demographic and existing level of skill, external pressures from Ofsted inspections or trust-wide policy will provide the parameters for PD decisions, PD leads do not have to start with a blank slate.

In their excellent paper, 'Effective teacher professional development', Sims, et al. (2022) reported findings of a meta-analysis of 104 studies into effective PD. The research team identified four essential ingredients of effective PD programmes:

1. enhance the knowledge of participants

2. help participants set clear goals

3. support participants in developing techniques for use in the classroom

4. help participants to embed the technique into their practice.

Within each of the four essential ingredients, they highlighted a set of mechanisms to support programme leaders and participants. We have outlined some of the mechanisms below, and encourage you to read the paper in full.

1a. Manage cognitive load of teachers

Given the limited capacity of working memory, it is important to consider how you are chunking up information for teachers and where you plan opportunities for deliberate practice. A secure understanding of the content and ample opportunity to practise applying it offers teachers the chance to self-check their understanding and ask for clarification when needed. Deliberate practice opportunities ensure a low stakes practise environment in which teachers can build their confidence with their new knowledge. This sends the powerful message that PD is about practise and improving, not complying. In this way, teachers sense they are accountable for engaging in the *process* of applying the new learning.

1b. Revisit material

Regularly revisiting material provides teachers with the opportunity to refresh their understanding but also to strengthen their command of new techniques or strategies. It engages accountability for process because by deliberately revisiting, PD leads are letting teachers know that forgetting is natural and improvement therefore may not be a neat upward trajectory. This contributes to psychological safety.

2a. Agree on a goal to direct teacher attention to the desired change

Teachers must commit to a goal that they will work towards. Teaching is cognitively demanding and so goals need to be granular to enable teachers to be able to focus their attention on a single, high-leverage practice that will improve their teaching. The success that they are likely to feel as a result feeds into their sense of psychological safety and allows them to experience the success of the process which in turn reinforces accountability to the process over the outcome.

2b. Reinforce the value of the practice

Subsequently reinforcing the value of the practice will also reinforce teachers' sense of security in applying it and therefore, the positive accountability to the goal of the process.

2c. Give evidence from a credible source

Taking an evidence-informed approach to the PD that you provide will not only guide you in how to think deeply about how to adapt programmes for your specific context, but it will also add to the psychological safety of teachers who will be more likely to trust in the efficacy of your initiative.

3a. Provide teachers with advice from colleagues

This should be focused on the granular improvement that you, as the lead, want teachers to make. This process removes ambiguity and the clarity that results is especially powerful in establishing psychological confidence and safety.

3b. Provide opportunities for modelling

There should be opportunities for modelling and this is particularly impactful when delivered by a more senior or experienced colleague. This breaks any sense of accountability only being in place to those above you. The more experienced colleague is accountable for the clarity of the modelling process and this positions them alongside the teacher rather than dictating from above.

3c. Provide opportunities for teachers to rehearse and deliver feedback

Following modelling, teachers should be given rehearsal time in a low stakes environment to iron out any disconnects between theoretical understanding and practical application. This is referred to as the 'knowing, doing gap' (Knight, 2013). The more rehearsal a teacher can do, the better and it should be followed by clear, actionable feedback to improve the next rehearsal.

4a. Action planning to embed techniques

If you want teachers to genuinely invest their time and energy into implementing the PD sessions you provide, make sure you build the kind of thinking you want them to do into the activities you ask of them. For example, if you want teachers to invest in identifying opportunities to check for understanding more effectively in lessons, get them to look at upcoming lessons and find the points at which they need to be certain of student understanding before moving on to the next stage of the lesson. Then, allow time to design, critique and improve questioning strategies that will reliably check that student understanding is clear.

Psychological safety is a product of the decisions and choices that leaders make. When it comes to the leadership of teacher development, designing a PD programme with the above principles in mind is not only more likely to have tangible impact on the quality of teaching in your school but it is also likely to reinforce a culture of practise, development and improvement which in turn contribute to psychological safety.

Instructional coaching

No PD programme would be complete without instructional coaching being at the heart of it. 'In terms of impact on student outcomes, instructional coaching has one of the strongest evidence bases of any form of CPD' (Farndon, 2019). Instructional coaching utilises deliberate practice to help teachers incrementally develop their teaching through a granular focus on aspects of their practice. Typically, it involves an observation of the teacher by an instructional coach followed by a feedback session which identifies a goal for improvement and looks at strategies and techniques to help achieve the goal. The teacher then settles on a technique or strategy that they want to master and then engages in cycles of modelling and rehearsal. As part of the most effective instructional coaching sessions, the coach will help the teacher to identify behaviours to always keep the target strategy front and centre of their thinking. This might be as simple as a visual prompt on a PowerPoint slide to remind the teacher to use a particular strategy at that point in the lesson.

While there are clear principles that are likely to make instructional coaching successful, it is also important to recognise that more expert teachers are likely to have a greater control over and understanding of their own development needs. Knight (2013) proposes the idea of a facilitative to directive continuum with more expert teachers taking on the role of expert when being coached as they are more likely able to accurately understand their own development needs. Conversely, novice teachers are more likely to require a more directive approach, similar to that written about by Bambrick-Santoyo (2016). When deciding on the approach, coaches need to base their decision on the individual context of the individual they are coaching. However, it is also important to note that, due to the cognitively demanding nature of teaching, even an experienced teacher may find it difficult to pay attention to diagnosing their own development within a lesson, rendering a more directive approach most appropriate.

Implementation challenges

As well as considering the relative expertise of each teacher, PD leads must also consider other contextual challenges when leading a teacher development programme based on a model of instructional coaching. Consider how skilled your coaching team really is. Being an expert teacher does not necessarily make you a good coach. A thorough understanding of the principles of impactful instructional coaching outlined above is essential before someone begins coaching. So, absolutely invest time and resources in training coaches.

Having said that expert teachers do not always make expert coaches, it is also important to acknowledge that unlike some other forms of coaching where expertise in the field is not necessary, in instructional coaching (literally coaching of instruction) domain expertise is required. That is to say that an ineffective teacher is not the appropriate person to provide instructional coaching for colleagues. This is a key contextual factor for Deputy Heads in charge of teacher development, especially when considering a peer-to-peer coaching model.

The size of your school is another key implementation challenge. How many people will need coaching to fulfil the needs of the whole staff? Do you have that many teachers who are willing and have the capacity to train to become effective coaches?

Consider your school culture when devising your implementation plan. One of the most positive impacts I have seen on school culture has been schools where every teacher is a coach as well as a mentee. This reduces the sense of upward accountability and creates a sense of shared responsibility for the development of teaching in the school. However, for this to be impactful, coach training must ensure that every member of staff has the knowledge and understanding of how to deliver great instructional coaching. So, if you want to harness the cultural impact of this model, be ready to invest heavily in developing your coaches.

Confidentiality is key. Teachers need to know that details of observations and coaching sessions are not being fed back to the Headteacher for the purpose of their evaluation. Regardless of your context, if you want development to prevail, make sure you offer psychological safety to allow people to focus on it.

'Nothing works everywhere but everything works somewhere' (Wiliam, 2018). Let's explore that in the context of instructional coaching. Contextual features such as school size, staff expertise and to what extent the leader is concerned with cultural impact, are all valid considerations and will likely differ from school to school. However, the fundamental features of PD identified by Sims et al. (2022) are the ingredients which are likely to give your instructional coaching programme the greatest impact. Before we leave instructional coaching behind, Josh Goodrich, founder of the StepLab instructional coaching platform and former Vice Principal for Professional Development, has provided a valuable professional perspective on instructional coaching and its practical application.

PROFESSIONAL PERSPECTIVE

By Josh Goodrich – CEO StepLab, an evidence-based professional development programme designed for schools and teachers that helps implement instructional coaching.

There's a difference between believing – as I do – that great PD is at the heart of transformative school leadership, and asserting that there is a single, right way to do it. While the recent focus on the power of PD in UK education has been welcome, it brings with it inevitable claims that there is only one way to get things right.

Countering this, we would argue that schools that run effective professional development follow in the teachings of Led Zeppelin, adopting what might be called a 'tight but loose' approach. By 'tight', we mean a deliberate focus on embedding the essential, evidence-based active ingredients of effective PD - such as sustained duration, content focus, opportunities for collaboration and iterative practice (Sims et al., 2021). The 'loose' refers to the school's ability to adapt and rework these ingredients to its unique culture, context and staff needs. The balance between structure and flexibility is crucial: too much rigidity can stifle relevance, while too much freedom risks incoherence.

Tight: Which aspects of their PD programme should leaders keep 'tight'?

Mechanism-rich

There is compelling evidence that effective PD contains a balance of some important 'active ingredients': instilling knowledge, setting goals, developing technical practices and embedding through practice (Goodrich, 2024; Sims et al., 2022).

Any PD programme should take care to ensure that they are operating a 'balanced design', where teachers encounter as many of these active mechanisms as possible, as often as possible.

Component-rich

As powerful as instructional coaching is as a teacher learning tool, it's important not to fetishise it. Coaching is very good at supporting teachers to make consistent improvements, but it doesn't form the complete PD picture.

The holy trinity of PD components is:

- group rehearsal
- instructional coaching
- and co-planning.

Used well, these three components align vertically to provide teachers with a complete map of how, when and why to implement new strategies successfully. New practices are introduced, explained, modelled and rehearsed through whole-staff group rehearsal. These same techniques are adapted to fit subject or phase through co-planning in smaller teams. Finally, instructional coaching can be used to support teachers to implement successfully where it counts: in the classroom.

Laser-focused

From a teacher's perspective, the education system is 'noisy' (Kennedy, 2016). Teachers are often faced with multiple, conflicting perspectives on what they should be focusing on, some coming from school leaders, others from external sources like the government and social media. On top of this, teacher's internal lives are equally 'noisy': teaching is busy, at times stressful and comes with a high cognitive load.

As leaders of PD, it is our job to quiet this noise, ensuring that teachers are able focus on one granular, precise thing at a time. Equally, it is our job to ensure that teachers encounter important new ideas and practices with regularity and rhythm rather than through a 'one and done' approach.

Loose: Which aspects of PD programme should be 'loose'?

Implementation journey

One of my foundational beliefs is that every teacher deserves regular coaching for the length of their career. This doesn't mean that I think that every school should make this happen *now*. Indeed, I think rushing towards this end point is likely to be an error.

The journey towards high-impact PD should be taken slowly, carefully and with a route that is bespoke to context. Some schools may need to build culture over time through zero-stakes positive drop-ins; some will need to focus on building a culture of modelling and deliberate practice through group rehearsal; others may need to work almost exclusively on teachers' curricular knowledge; yet others may want to start working on coaching using 'expert' coaches, or with their entire teams; finally, many schools may wish to use a combination of the above.

Importantly, there are no 'right' or 'wrong' answers. The only thing that matters is that leaders are plugged into where their school is, what's happening now, whether it's working and where they might want to go next.

Selecting effective teaching practices

We are bombarded by information about evidence-based, effective teaching. It can feel to school leaders like if they don't implement the entire of *Teach Like a Champion* (Lemov, 2010) and Rosenshine's (1986) principles this instant, they are failing.

I think the most effective PD leaders, however, take a 'loose' approach to the selection of focus practices. For some schools, the right approach may be to open up a large selection of practices to the discretion of coaches. For others, it may be more appropriate to select a single practice as the focus for all staff, building up a knowledge of effective teaching as a team.

Conclusion

There is no single method of implementing great PD. There are no quick fixes, or short cuts. There are no silver bullets.

PD leaders do, however, have a responsibility to be plugged into the best available evidence about how to support teachers to learn. In this, they must be 'tight'.

They also have a responsibility to use this information in a way that best suits their context, and to remain constantly alive to the need to change it up. In this, they must be 'loose'.

Key takeaways

- Establish psychological safety by truly committing to a culture of development and improvement and separating it from judgement and evaluation.

- Accountability is rooted in relationships and as such should be the product of conversations rather than directives from leaders.

- Model shared accountability as the Deputy Head, by taking on a small action that binds you to the success or failure of a particular initiative.

In this chapter we've highlighted the importance of accountability to process rather than outcome and the positive influence this has on teacher motivation. We examined the efficacy of instructional coaching and reflected on how this approach to teacher development can harness what the research tells us makes the most effective PD.

Hopefully the professional perspectives and case studies, along with the reflection points, have allowed you to reflect on the extent to which your own context influences how you will apply these principles in your current or future roles. The central challenge of leading teacher development is defined by the paradoxical nature of having to ensure improvement for the good of students at the same time as providing developmental training opportunities for staff. The thing that goes across contexts that binds together practice in all schools and situations is the concept of decency. Believing that every teacher is capable of and deserves great PD and that consistent, evidence-informed approaches across a school will deliver that. A genuine commitment to improving teaching for students ensures you can take pride in reflecting on your practice, where decency is at the heart of your role.

7

Developing leaders

Your leadership – in whatever form it currently takes – may extend to identifying, nurturing and empowering the next generation of educational leaders within your school. Approach your privileged position with respect and decency whereby the sense of achievement with a successful transition or promotion is worth the hours of preparation and coaching.

Leadership, at its core, extends beyond personal development; it is about advancing the entire institution collectively. In this chapter, we delve into the methods by which you can ignite and steer the journey of emerging leaders, equipping them with the essential resources, insights and mentorship required for their growth. Through case studies and school-based scenarios, we will delve into strategies aimed at refining the capabilities of seasoned leaders, ensuring they stay agile and adaptable in the ever-shifting terrain of education.

The hidden leader

Spotting leadership potential in a member of staff is one of education's great joys. Yet leadership traits are many and nuanced. Northouse (2018) describes leadership as having 'definitional issues' (p. 45), which centre around the concept that individuals working together towards some form of common goal or aim, will be influenced by the process of leadership (p. 43).

You know a leader when you see one: the teacher who volunteers their time or knowledge in staff briefing, the teacher who is excelling in their own practice to the degree that other teachers seek them out for guidance; that one person whose opinion carries more weight than others and to whose side others gather in times of crisis.

Whilst gut instinct plays a huge role in determining which of our staff would be most suited to a leadership role, Figure 12 identifies those key features that all potential leaders have in common:

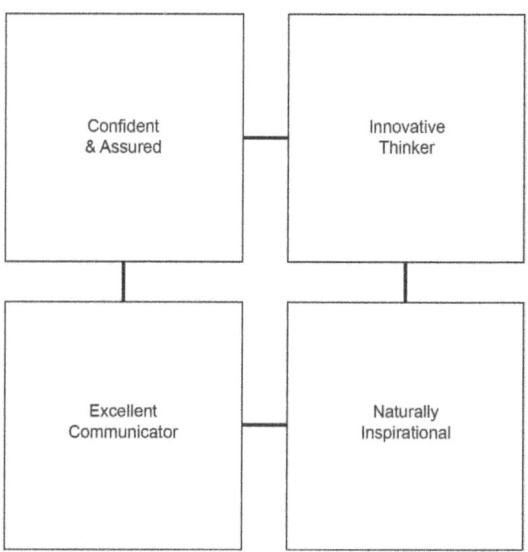

FIGURE 12: *Commonalities of good leadership*

These four attributes could read exactly like the desirable attributes in a teacher advertisement. The skills above form the backbone of excellent teaching practice. Let's unpick what we specifically mean with regards to our commonalities of good leadership:

Confident and assured

- **You have self-belief:** A confident leader has a strong sense of self-belief and demonstrates trust in their own abilities and decisions. This type of self-assurance is a critical element of confident leadership when making tough decisions and guiding others in your team and beyond.

- **You are calm under pressure:** Stability and reassurance is the best kind of side effect of confident leaders when faced with challenging situations; they exude an of air calm, cool and collected emotions that steadies the ship.

- **You have a presence:** Confident leaders can't help but command respect and attention if they find themselves in the right environment. This assured sense of self is essential for delivering effective communications to a variety of stakeholders.

Innovative thinker

- **You are creative:** Thinking 'outside the box' is a classic trope of creative people and extends into leadership. Coming up with creative solutions and alternative options when presented with problems is a brilliant way to endear yourself to a team and discover new ways to achieve goals.

- **You are adaptable:** Being open to change and willing to adapt quickly to new situations is utterly vital when considering qualities of leadership. Sarah Cottinghatt's work in adaptive expertise (2024) investigates the concept of mental models and how they are used by expert leaders and teachers to adapt in the moment to their given complex circumstances. Indeed, being able to creatively identify the aim and goal within the desired change is a step we cannot afford to miss (Kohlbeck, 2024).

- **You are forward-thinking:** Innovative thinkers are blessed with the ability of always looking ahead. Planning for future challenges is as important as seeking avenues for new opportunities and provides this style of leadership with a sense of responsibility for the future of school.

Excellent communicator

- **You have clarity:** Excellent communicators are able to convey ideas, concepts and instructions clearly. This level of professional clarity – planned in advance – ensures that everyone is able to understand and take part in the vision and objectives being communicated.

- **You actively listen:** Hearing and listening are two very different styles of paying attention: inattentive and attentive. If you actively listen then you are responding immediately thereby valuing their input and fostering an environment of open communication.

- **You are persuasive:** As a skilled communicator, you can use your attentive and active skills to persuade and motivate others. Building consensus and 'buy-in' is so much more than checking in with everyone – it's about clear communication at the start of a process of change and transition which, if done correctly, will drive action.

Naturally inspirational

- **You are motivational:** You will observe inspirational leaders motivating and energising their teams, instilling a sense of purpose and passion for their work in any area of the school or organisation.

- **You are a role model:** Leading by example is one of the best ways to inspire others to behave and think in a way that is beneficial for your setting. Explicitly demonstrating the values and behaviours you want to see will positively inspire those around you.

- **You have vision:** Whether it's from your Headteacher or from your own motivations, inspirational leaders have a clear vision. This vision is articulated in a way that, much like the idea of a role model, inspires others to join you in pursuing it: it needn't be flashy or too simple, instead clarity of vision means chunked steps of progress that can be quickly identified and evaluated.

CASE STUDY: SONIA

Sonia was a highly qualified French and German language teacher. Very often, her mood was a dominating force in the staff room and the mood of others was influenced heavily by hers. Sonia's knowledge of evidence-based pedagogy was superb and other teachers often sought her out for her opinion. She was respected, regarded highly and very ambitious.

Senior Leadership had observed these positive attributes and, with promotion in mind, approached Sonia

> with a Middle Leadership role in teaching and learning pedagogy across the school. She was informed that her communication skills, subject knowledge and obvious respect from staff were all attributes suited to the role. Without any hesitation, Sonia politely declined the promotion and substantial pay rise; she was more than happy with her current position.
>
> The SLT were stunned. Surely, they thought, Sonia was a natural born leader. Declining this position didn't make any sense. Their plan to upskill their teaching staff through Sonia's promotion was now dead in the water and Sonia was none the wiser.

The 'want' of leadership

Sonia's story speaks to a wider narrative of the 'want' for a position of leadership and how this must be present in order for a complete buy-in to a position that will inevitably bring stress and responsibility above and beyond those experienced by teaching staff. Assuming that Sonia is content with her current position and that leadership doesn't interest her at all, is there anything the leadership of the school could have done to either make Sonia aware of their plans and to avoid their own embarrassment at their assumption of her aspiration?

The SLT's mistake was to assume that leadership would be the inevitable goal for Sonia. There was perhaps a lack of decency in their approach which came across as self-serving or simply in the best interest of the school rather than the individual. The assumption that anyone would jump at the chance to be a leader reflected a certain oversight or misjudgement on their part. A better approach might have been an internal leadership coaching programme that develops those with the desire to be leaders to access mentors and training within school. They could have asked Sonia what might make her role feel even more fulfilling and acted on her response instead. Six months later, they tried a different approach. Instead of offering Sonia a promotion, they asked: 'What would make your role here even more fulfilling?' Her answer surprised them: she wanted to mentor new teachers but had no interest in formal management responsibilities. So, Sonia became the school's Lead Teaching Mentor – a role that made use of her natural leadership qualities without requiring the administrative and strategic responsibilities she didn't want. She flourished, the new teachers benefited enormously and the school gained a crucial development resource.

The big question here is: why don't schools do this kind of PD more regularly outside of funding a National Professional Qualification (NPQ)? Cost is a factor, but hypothetically – and rather idealistically – remove that element for a second and let's consider why. Is it because if schools set up a coaching programme and someone graduates from that into SLT then their success or otherwise is a joint responsibility of them and those who coached them? We would argue that the decent action is to assume that exact shared responsibility and the vulnerability that comes with it. If, through this process, a member of staff then moves schools to further enhance their career then the process has been successful. We will explore monitoring and accountability in the next chapter.

Next steps: nurturing leadership

What do the SLT do to nurture that leader? It's important to avoid using promotion as a carrot that works Sonia into the ground; it's about ensuring that she is nurtured into the role rather than thrust into it. Is all of this pointless if leadership is not something to which she aspires? An enforced natural leader who resents the job will not experience longevity in the role or indeed be successful in leading anything and will, eventually, pale in comparison compared to a natural leader who has been coached and mentored into the role. All of these questions come from a place of decency; from putting the person before the school. Yet in doing so, the school benefits from a motivated well-supported leader. Some may describe this approach therefore as the sweet spot in a key paradox of leadership: how does a leader remain relentlessly focused on the development of the organisation, while simultaneously patiently nurturing the people within it. The bridge between the personal and the transactional can be established through identifying and building the 'want'.

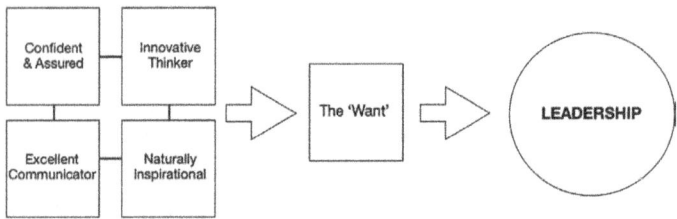

FIGURE 13: *Commonalities in the journey to leadership*

Removing 'the want' from the journey to leadership leaves the destination nearly impossible to reach. There are, however, situations where reluctant leaders, thrust into positions of power with very little choice, can do well. Take, for instance, a recent situation where Tracey, the Assistant Principal for Inclusion, became Acting Deputy Head after the sudden resignation of the Head Teacher and the subsequent promotion of the Deputy. Tracey was very happy with her role and the context of her particular school was that the Deputy had oversight of academic progress. With such a sudden change in leadership, Tracey had very little choice but to embrace her new role. She flourished and found that 'the want' was something that evolved and developed over time, having previously turned down opportunities to lead with more responsibility.

Research point: reluctant leaders

In a 2014 research study conducted by London's Cass Business School, a compelling insight emerged: reluctant leaders possess distinct qualities that can profoundly impact organisational dynamics for the better (Hempson, 2014). These individuals, often thrust into leadership positions after having earned their stripes through diligent work in the trenches, exhibit a unique ability to navigate the intricate realm of office politics while simultaneously fostering an atmosphere of autonomy.

One of the standout findings of this study was legitimacy in leadership, or the acceptance and endorsement of a leader by their followers. Reluctant leaders tend to garner a higher degree of perceived legitimacy among their colleagues and subordinates. This legitimacy stems from their history of hard work and dedication within the organisation, which establishes them as credible and trustworthy figures in the eyes of their peers. They are, crucially, someone who has walked with their colleagues, felt their struggles and their emotions in their roles and so is likely to bring decency to their leadership practice as a result.

The key takeaway from this research is: when it comes to selecting a leader, it's essential to look beyond the individuals who actively seek the role. While eager candidates may bring enthusiasm and ambition, those who require a bit of persuasion to step into leadership roles should not be dismissed. Reluctant leaders often possess the invaluable combination of experience, credibility, and the ability to balance control with promoting autonomy within the team.

It's important to recognise leadership potential in those who may not be overtly vying for the position. Their reticence might reflect their humility and decency, a trait that can be a valuable asset in fostering collaboration and maintaining a harmonious work environment.

How does this apply?

The application of these findings to the school environment is quite obvious when you consider some of the language often used in staff rooms: the 'us and them' attitude to SLT, leaders referring to 'the troops' or working on the 'front line'. We've all experienced the senior leaders who are parachuted into schools with little knowledge of your context and who manage to annoy everyone simply because of their position. It is not possible to transfer your own leadership style from one school to another (Miller, 2018, p.121) and so we're less likely to see success from this kind of leader if they don't adapt to their new context.

Leaders that emerge from the staff body are far more likely to be lifted and supported by their peers and therefore experience longevity in role. Even those reluctant to lead are likely to do well due to their attitude towards the job. It's not entirely healthy but many teachers we work with, and have spoken to, see their job as a 'calling' or vocation. This attitude is helpful to an unexpected leader because they are far more likely to accept pressures and conditions others in another profession may not in order to ensure the smooth running of the school.

We believe developing leaders is a skill that requires you to find 'the want' sooner rather than later so that it can be nurtured and empowered. Instantaneous rises to leadership may prove successful in the short term, but where's the decency in that?

To preserve our colleagues and friends, we need to make sure their 'want' is the attribute to be developed; we can't force it to be there or we risk creating problems and issues further down the line. To this end, unless key cultural changes are required at speed, leaders should be developed from within through a supported PD process that can foster 'the want' or otherwise seek out those that might be reluctant to lead. Educational leadership is a Janus-like balance of looking forwards and future planning whilst simultaneously looking back to ensure you're being followed in the right way and – crucially – by the right people.

Guy Shears, CEO and Executive Principal of the Central Region Schools Trust, offers his experience in identifying potential leaders.

PROFESSIONAL PERSPECTIVE

By Guy Shears – CEO and Executive Principal of the Central Region Schools Trust

There are several factors crucial for identifying potential new leaders. We take a systematic approach in our organisation and review our staff every six months, assessing:

- Current performance. If someone is new to the role, we will support them to become as good as possible, as quickly as possible.
- Future potential. We look at whether someone might be 'two steps, five years ready', for instance, a current middle leader, with the right investment, may move in that time scale from their current role, through Assistant Headship through to starting Deputy Headship. We also

assess who is 'one step, two years ready', for instance, a Deputy Headteacher who, with the right investment, might be ready for Headship in two years.
- Integrity. It is important that people don't rush to gain the next promotion, and are not simply wanting the title or pay increase of a Deputy Headteacher job. Instead, I look for people who strive to do great work, day in day out, driven by the inherent value in doing a great job.
- Loyalty to the school they currently work at, and to the post they hold. There seems to be a trend of get a job, get up to speed for a year, do the job well for a year, and then spend the next year trying to get the next job. It is reassuring when professionals take the time to get up to speed, and then do the job better and better over a longer period, taking every opportunity to develop themselves in the role so that they are 'ripe' for the next step, not rushing to get the next one.

Some of the very best executive leaders have moved from Assistant Headteacher, through Deputy Headteacher, and then Headteacher, to an executive role, across a seven-to-ten-year period. They have always had specific areas of expertise but have also taken on areas of leadership outside of their comfort zone, learning the full remit of the next step, and especially for headship. Once they are very secure in headship, then the hard graft of running more than one school has a strong chance of success. In my own development, as a Deputy Headteacher in a Birmingham secondary in the early 2000s, I was asked by Brighouse to take on a headship in a school that was struggling. It was flattering, but I felt I wasn't ready. I didn't want to take on the responsibility before I knew I had enough knowledge to deliver and instead took a two year secondment as deputy at a school in a very difficult context with high percentages of children experiencing deprivation. By the time I secured a headship, I was much more 'ripe', although looking back, still not fully ready!

In modern Trust structures, I feel that there is misunderstanding in the belief that executive headship is somehow easier than headship. This is so far from the truth, but I think is perhaps a testimony to those Executive Heads I have had the privilege to lead, who give the impression to their colleagues that the job is easy. The tough stuff and the long hours are kept well hidden. There is nothing worse to me than a leader who absorbs energy telling people how hard they work. The volume and quality of output, and the clear benefits to pupils and staff, will speak for themselves when leadership is authentic.

In terms of the attributes of character that are vital, confidence is important. Resilience, matched with humour, are vital. Authentic empathy for pupils, colleagues, community and in life in general is essential. It helps if one is likeable, and certainly any individual needs to be respectful, and command respect.

In terms of behaviours, we look for alignment to our culture. In particular, a passion to our mission of 'supporting social justice through exceptional school'. Interviews are a two-way process, and schools and trusts are very different, so are not right for every individual. In short, someone may be ready to be a great Deputy Headteacher, but they may not fit our culture. Equally, we may see someone fitting our culture, but it may not feel right to them. In both instances, it simply won't work, and that is a good thing.

These are the behaviours I believe develop strong climate, and, over time, strong culture. They are a strong checklist for all of us to self-assess against, and these are what I use when identifying talent.

Prioritise the success of our young people at all times

All members of the CENTRAL community advocate for the children and make decisions with our young people at heart. We have the highest expectations of all pupils and understand the importance of showing them how to achieve the habits that will lead them to success.

Be a role model

All staff are responsible for building our culture, trust and credibility. All members of the community need to walk the talk – all of the time. We all need to lead by example.

Communicate effectively

Staff need to be direct, honest, act with integrity and communicate appropriately all of the time. We look for honest, timely and professional face-to-face communication as a priority.

Keep your promises and stick to your organisational commitments

The importance of professional integrity is paramount. We need to aim to keep our word around our organisational commitments.

Commit to the development of others

People are our most valuable asset. We seek people who commit to our own professional growth in order to improve the outcomes for pupils. Line management support is vital to leadership – I will always explore the commitment to this as a high priority and what excellent looks like in line management support.

Have a solution-focused approach

Leaders need a positive can-do mindset and seek well-thought-through and appropriate solutions to problems.

Demonstrate full commitment to the bigger picture

Colleagues need to demonstrate loyalty, and to challenge each other appropriately and support each other at all times. We show flexibility and a willingness to be adaptable or, where necessary, compromise.

No one can manage all these, all day every day. We all have 'bad day' behaviours. Leaders being aware of these, knowing the impact of good day behaviours and being aware of their strategies to minimise bad day behaviours are a useful window into leadership potential.

I look for leaders who can demonstrate how their leadership to date has made a difference to young people's lives, *with* other people, and who have made mistakes and have learned from them. They come in many shapes and sizes, from ECTs through to executive leaders, from IT apprentices through to the C-Suite executives, they all embody this. We seek to identify them at every level, and to invest heavily in their development as we plan succession at every level of the organisation in the interests of the pupils now and into the future.

The ambitious leader

Having identified potential future leaders who have expressed their ambitions to progress – how do you develop their skills?

Provide leadership opportunities

The best lessons are taught in situ; decisions that leaders make on a daily, or hourly, basis can be workshopped and discussed but the key to the role is how they act in any given situation. The best way, therefore, for future leaders to develop is to experience those situations in a real context, which is much easier said than done. The challenge is how to balance the instinct driven decision making with the deep desire to 'get it right', to make the right call. One answer to this paradoxical challenge lies in the understanding and application of an agreed set of principles. Creating a set of guidelines for the ambitious leader will enable them to lead as their authentic selves while at the same time, remaining consistent with the organisational values currently in place.

The obvious route here might not be the best: titles and job roles automatically come with leadership responsibilities but giving these out for the experience alone isn't good practice. For instance, roles involving high-stakes outcomes such as SEND or safeguarding need to be considered carefully and shouldn't be treated as opportunities for ambition or experimentation.

CASE STUDY: DAVID

David was looking for leadership opportunities and asked for some safeguarding experience as he had an interest in this area. The senior leaders decided to offer David the chance to train as a Deputy Designated Safeguarding Lead (DDSL).

David jumped at the chance and was eager to prove himself with this new-found position. It wasn't long before the SLT was alerted to a change of attitude from David, turning from eagerness to arrogance. Before completing sufficient training, he was using his new title to conduct learning walks and observe safeguarding practices in classrooms without full knowledge of the DSL proper or the teaching staff. Unions started to get involved in response to the unplanned observations and teaching staff were, understandably, not happy with this level of scrutiny from someone so new to the position.

Before David was called into a meeting about his conduct, he handled a disclosure from a student reporting potential abuse at home. Full of his own sense of self and the importance of the job, David called the child's parents to arrange a meeting. Luckily, the DSL managed to catch up on the situation and spoke to the *Multi-*Agency Safeguarding Hub (MASH) team with the local authority who gave step-by-step guidance on how to proceed; David had not told the parents why the meeting was needed.

To ease your mind, the disclosure was resolved immediately, and both the child and family were supported. But David's eagerness to lead mixed with his naivety in the role likely put a child at risk.

David's case is compelling because there may have been a missed opportunity to avoid this situation. It is laudable that David used the PD route to seek out leadership opportunities and to specify his area of interest. Doubtless, the leadership of the school jumped at the opportunity having spotted 'the want' in David but developing him as leader in this field so quickly put a child at risk. Safeguarding is not an area into which you 'dip a toe' and stretch your leadership legs. David was due much more support and training but his desire to have a responsibility above and beyond his teaching duties clouded both his judgement and that of his leadership team.

In the day-to-day reality of school life, leadership opportunities are not easily accessible due to the constraints we are all too familiar with: time, money, space. We would argue, however, that providing leadership opportunities that have real and measurable outcomes will bring dividends far greater than an initial outlay of the aforementioned constraints.

LEADERSHIP OPPORTUNITY SUGGESTIONS

- Organising a school trip
- Running a club/homework intervention
- Leading on enrichment across the school – clubs, events, speaker and trips
- Leading the support for an under-performing year group
- Mentoring a trainee or Early Career Teacher
- Leading a subject and monitoring your own impact
- Leading workshops for parents and carers
- Leading work towards an award or accreditation
- Leading a whole-school project: climate, environment, charitable causes

Foster collaboration

Depending on the size of your setting, you're likely to want – or even need – a multitude of leadership roles developing at the same time. Running a school in any context involves a set of uniquely complicated machinations and one of those is the leadership team working together towards a shared set of goals. If you use a Self Evaluation Form or School Improvement Plan then many of the leadership targets will be based around those requirements. However, your emerging and ambitious leaders should be given the opportunities to work together through team projects or in a mentorship/coaching programme.

Encourage innovation

If your ambitious leaders possess 'the want' of the role, they are also far more likely to be interested in their own development and PD – this is a trait you will be well-placed to utilise. By giving them the opportunity to suggest their own mini projects or outcomes, you already have an individual invested in the outcomes through progress you can measure. Your context will set certain limits and restrictions but by encouraging 'out of the box' thinking through supportive conversations during dedicated development time, this demonstrates a sense of decency that will be appreciated.

Lead by example

Hopefully, if leadership is an area you are interested in, then it will be reflected in the culture of your setting and will encourage innovation and growth. The freedom to demonstrate your own leadership style and personal beliefs will be key in confidently demonstrating to others the leadership you wish to see around you. If we are to accept that the best leaders for your school will evolve from within then they need to have had prolonged exposure to your positive influence around the school.

Some actions you could consider taking:

- Demonstrate your own excellence by showing consistency and dedication to your role(s) as it exists.

- Have your own goals by demonstrating your commitment to your own development through courses, qualifications and PD.

- Model effective communication by being clear and transparent, as well demonstrating active listening skills whilst being open to engage in honest and potentially difficult conversations.

- Empathy is hugely important when looking at a leadership approach of decency and sharing some of your responsibilities with another member of the team will allow them to experience some of the excitement and responsibility of leadership without putting any outcomes – or children – at risk.

- Demonstrate critical thinking and encourage it in your everyday practice. Those staff members who mirror these behaviours and skills will themselves begin to find genuine moments of analysis that result in solutions to complex problems.

- Be authentically you and actively choose to show particular vulnerabilities at specific times to reveal to others that leadership is not always perfect; that leaders have flaws and can still be effective.

> **PERSONAL REFLECTION**
>
> Can you think of a time when you used your position to lead by example and saw a positive impact on your team?
>
> _____
> _____
> _____
> _____
> _____

Be supportive

Yet another obvious one? Maybe, but the middle leaders and Deputy Heads we have spoken to mentioned the other paradox in developing leaders and that's the odious nature of sink or swim vs micromanagement. Where leadership development often fails is when the concept of trust is so openly rejected and any opportunity for the leader to flourish is dampened by a senior leader ensuring nothing can go wrong. Putting this into a classroom setting, how on earth is anyone to learn if they don't have the capacity – or the psychological safety – to make errors? Naturally, our jobs have outcomes that can have major ramifications in our school communities but that's where we can show some decency and give appropriate leadership opportunities at levels in which the leader can flourish and succeed.

Many of the leaders we have spoken to have only ever experienced the extreme ends of the spectrum:

a) *'You're on your own – good luck!'* – a sink or swim attitude from senior leadership that provides no relevant PD or training where the risk of making a mistake is disproportionately weighed against them.

Instead, look for: *'You're the leader and I trust you to make change but what do you need from me?'*

or

b) *'You're the leader in title but I'll tell you when to breathe'* – micromanagement of their every move ensures risk of error is entirely mitigated.

Instead, look for: *'How would you like us to work together so that you feel supported in your autonomy around the role?'*

Neither of these approaches is suitable for sustained and successful leadership development as they reveal the leadership of the school to care for the institution over the people. Both options demonstrate a disregard for the skills that the leader can bring through natural ability that needs training and nurturing not ignoring completely.

These suggestions are just a few among many practical approaches and there are undoubtedly numerous other strategies that can foster the development of future leaders from your unique position in the school. It is vital, however, to understand that all these recommendations share a common core principle: your actions and the manner in which you carry them out really do matter. In the context of leadership development, actions speak louder than words and how leadership opportunities are established, how individuals are mentored and how collaboration is encouraged all profoundly influence the school's culture. Therefore, the commitment to decency, empathy and integrity in developing leaders is an absolute necessity for the growth and prosperity of both individuals and the entire school community.

8

Developing yourself

While self-development has been explored throughout this book, this chapter focuses specifically on you as Deputy Head. Teacher development efficacy has been empirically proven to improve not only the individual's performance, but also that of their students (Van de Brande and Zuccollo, 2021). It stands to reason, therefore, that your own development should be centre stage. Our joint desire for crafting our own PD has created a journey that is in and of itself fulfilling and beneficial to our careers, our schools and, by extension, the students.

As you explore your own development, it is time to think strategically and with purpose.

In Chapter 7 we addressed developing leaders and spoke about the need for 'the why' and how. Without it, leadership would be impossible to develop even if a teacher showed potential. It is slightly different for us as existing leaders because we have already identified our own 'why' which explains our current position in our schools. But it would be foolish to think that such an idea wasn't ephemeral or variable to the extreme. Assessment of our own 'why' would almost certainly identify changes in motivation and purpose.

> **PERSONAL REFLECTION**
>
> Think back to why you pursued the position of Deputy Head. Can you remember what it was? Has it changed since then and can you identify it now?
>
> _____
> _____
> _____
> _____
> _____

Establishing your own 'why' in this moment will allow you to begin to identify the most appropriate route for your development. Fullan (2007) identified several states of emotional competence in individuals that might bring about substantive and meaningful change. Some of those that we feel are key to your own career development are labelled by Fullan as self-awareness, self-regulation and motivation.

> **PROFESSIONAL PERSPECTIVE**
>
> *By Richard Skilbeck – Director of Music and Assistant Head of Sixth Form at Edgbaston High School for Girls*
>
> The path from Music Teacher and Choirmaster to Director of Music (DoM) is both a rewarding and challenging journey, marked by expanding responsibilities and evolving identity. This progression within a school music department requires adapting to diverse roles, managing

a large team, and balancing administrative duties with musical and pedagogical leadership.

As a Deputy DoM, I was afforded the opportunity to learn many facets of the Director role without assuming full responsibility. I managed visiting music teachers and oversaw certain curriculum responsibilities across the prep school, senior school and sixth form, developing essential administrative skills and broadening my pedagogical scope. However, stepping into the DoM role brought a fundamental shift, moving from hands-on involvement to a broader strategic and managerial focus. Where I had once 'done' much of the teaching and organising myself, I now needed to delegate effectively; an adjustment that called for building trust within my team and relinquishing some direct control.

In this new role, I found myself leading a large and diverse department composed of both full-time and part-time staff, including visiting music teachers and additional specialist educators. Managing such a team required not only logistical coordination but also sensitivity to the unique contributions of each individual. This restructuring also altered the department's dynamic, as I now served as a mentor and facilitator rather than a peer, supporting and empowering others to achieve success.

The responsibilities of a DoM extend beyond the music curriculum and concert programming to encompass additional areas such as managing London Academy of Music and Dramatic Art (LAMDA) examinations within the school. Incorporating this into my role added another layer of complexity, necessitating a balance of logistical planning, academic oversight, and strategic direction. Managing LAMDA requires not only aligning it with the department's goals but also ensuring its seamless integration into the school's overall educational framework, offering students a holistic approach to performance and communication skills.

In addition, I am tasked with adapting my teaching approach across a wide age range, from the youngest in prep school to sixth form students at A Level. Each age group presents unique educational needs and challenges, requiring flexibility and an understanding of developmental stages in music education. Teaching prep students demands a playful, exploratory approach to foster initial musical enthusiasm, while A Level students require a more rigorous, analytical style, preparing them for advanced study or performance. Balancing these different demands is central to my role, ensuring that each student receives age-appropriate instruction that nurtures their growth.

One personal challenge on this journey has been maintaining a sense of my own identity as a musician within the school. As administrative and leadership responsibilities increase, there is a risk of feeling distanced from the core musical activities that once defined my role. My identity as a performer, accompanist, or choirmaster sometimes becomes overshadowed by managerial duties, leading to moments of reflection on my role's changing nature. Maintaining this personal connection to music is vital, both for my own fulfilment and to inspire students and colleagues authentically.

As the DoM, I strive to embody a servant leadership approach, focusing on enabling the success of students and staff within the department. Celebrating others' achievements has become a central part of my role – whether it's a student's successful concert performance or a staff member's innovative teaching approach. This shift from personal accomplishment to collective success

> underscores the transformation in my leadership style. By creating a supportive, collaborative environment, I aim to nurture each individual's strengths and encourage a sense of shared purpose within the department.
>
> Leading a music department requires adaptability, vision, and a balance of academic, creative, and logistical skills. As I continue to navigate this role, I remain committed to fostering a department that values excellence, creativity, and mutual support, while also preserving the joy and passion for music that initially inspired my career in education.

Richard's perspective offers us a window into the ever-evolving nature of the successful leader and ultimately, Deputy Head. The role is never static but dynamic and fluid, challenging your existing skill set to the very ends of its existence and then extending it that bit further than you had previously conceived were possible. As the role changes, you also need to adapt. Accompanying an adaptive approach with deep and tangible positivity will set the tone, not only for yourself but for those who follow your leadership.

A key strategy for helping you adapt to the shifting landscape of your role as well as to equip you with the new skill set you need, is to strategically pursue your own PD, as we will explore in more detail later on in this chapter.

There are myriad reasons for why you might consider PD that fall into those categories:

DEVELOPMENT MOTIVATORS

- Salary increase
- Desire for more responsibility
- Improving your own understanding to benefit your students
- Seeking new challenges.

Before embarking on any paid PD, it is important to consider both the benefits and drawbacks to what can often feel like a saturated area. Certainly, you would be hard-pressed to find a selection of interviewees for headship or promotion without one of the following post-nominals:

Course/ Qualification	Benefits	Drawbacks
NPQSL (National Professional Qualification for Senior Leadership) or NPQH (National Professional Qualification for Headship)	A nationally recognised qualification offers a benchmarked verification of your leadership knowledge and know-how.	Broad ranging content and skills. Can lack context specific application.
Master's Degree (e.g. MA in Education, MSc in Educational Leadership)	Likely exposure to financial compliance. An opportunity to engage in action research which could position you as uniquely research engaged.	Time consuming and homework heavy.

Course/ Qualification	Benefits	Drawbacks
Chartered Status (e.g., Chartered Teacher, Chartered Manager)	The quality of material on this course is exceptional and this allows you access to a body of knowledge that will no doubt further your thinking.	Fewer opportunities for interaction with other candidates.
Doctorate (PhD or EdD in Education)	The opportunity to research in depth and with expertise, a specific area of education is one that yields not only interesting findings but also the opportunity to become a genuine industry expert in a particular field.	Expensive and takes a long time to complete.

Develop your day-to-day

CASE STUDY: CHRIS AND ADAM

Chris hadn't anticipated, when chatting with Adam about podcast formats, that he would be rethinking not only his own practice as an English teacher, but a whole-school curriculum redesign.

> Adam pointed to an episode of Ollie Lovell's Education Research Reading Room (ERRR) with Sam Gibbs (see her professional perspective in Chapter 3) as an example of an excellent podcast with an interesting guest, high quality questioning and insightful educational takeaways. Sam had written a book with Zoe Hellman about concept-led English curricula and its potential impact on school systems that can be more flexible in their approach. In his own school Chris had struggled for some time to land on an approach for spring term exam season that didn't end up being filled with exam tips and tricks for Year 11 to get the best marks. He wanted a curriculum that addressed deeper meanings and spoke to students from much earlier in their school careers.
>
> Chris listened to the two episodes – nearly four hours of content – twice and then bought the book. He spent the following two months redesigning the English curriculum so that GCSE concepts were embedded from Year 5 onwards. A successful Ofsted inspection where reading and the strength of the English curriculum was praised as well as the best English results to date convinced him that this route was the right one.

This was a significant moment in Chris's teaching career that had been so geared towards leading others. A refocus on his personal teaching practice and beliefs lead him to a situation that required leadership skills but also a willingness to redefine his personal development that had a positive impact on the school and the success of the students.

PERSONAL REFLECTION

Can you remember your own hinge point? What was it? If it hasn't happened yet, how do you think you might find ways to grow and develop?

_____
_____
_____
_____
_____

PROFESSIONAL PERSPECTIVE

By Swabra Lloyd – Executive Headteacher, Forest Academy

Aligning ambition with strategic development is a vital component of career progression in the multifaceted role of a Deputy Headteacher. Understanding and committing to your 'why' provides the foundation needed to see development through, even when challenges arise. Clarifying career ambitions and addressing personal development gaps ensures growth remains aligned with your passions and keeps you motivated.

On my journey toward headship, it was crucial to expand my experience across various educational contexts. This deliberate choice allowed me to build situational leadership skills that proved invaluable. I worked in schools of varying sizes, both academies and maintained, across three local authorities. Each role offered a unique perspective on school operations – from rapid transformation to embedding excellence and navigating diverse socio-economic environments.

These varied experiences were both strategic and personal. They reduced any sense of imposter syndrome; having 'walked the walk' before 'talking the talk' reinforced my confidence to lead authentically. While some questioned why I didn't stay to see long-term results, my goal was clear: to grow continually as a leader and push beyond my comfort zone. Stagnation felt riskier than new challenges. This drive also led me to pursue a masters in Educational Leadership, aligning learning with my aspiration of leading entire school organisations.

Reflecting now on headship, I see how these experiences equipped me to adapt, strategise and lead effectively. Developing oneself must not be neglected amidst the competing priorities of a Deputy Headteacher's role. Maintaining focus on strategic personal development is essential. Reading widely, engaging with educational research, and exploring leadership insights beyond education enrich strategic thinking and adaptability. This approach fuels personal growth and fortifies leadership qualities.

Swabra's perspective offers us a timely reminder of the advantage of strategic self-development. Of course, development can happen by accident but it is so much richer, so much more purposeful and so much more worthwhile if you have sought a specific challenge to grow from yourself. It will allow you to remain in control of your own development in a role that so often places you on the treadmill of firefighting.

Beyond the assumption of headship

The prevailing assumption that every Deputy Head should pursue headship is not only misguided, it is potentially detrimental to both individual career satisfaction and the broader education system. The contemporary educational landscape offers unprecedented diversity in leadership opportunities, and successful self-development necessitates the alignment of professional growth with authentic aspirations rather than external expectations or perceived career hierarchies. Before engaging with any formal qualification or structured development opportunity, it is essential to conduct a rigorous assessment of your genuine leadership aspirations. This evaluation must be divorced from societal expectations, peer pressures, or assumptions about career progression, focusing instead on what constitutes meaningful professional fulfilment within your specific context and value system.

Governance opportunities

The hierarchy of leadership outlined in Chapter 1 (Figure 1) may make governance seem far removed from a Deputy Headteacher's daily role. Having spent so much time being cognisant of how to align with your Headteacher, seeing a school from the top-down might seem illogical. However, the best governing bodies 'develop strategy in the best interest of pupils and schools' (Clapham, 2024, p. 15), and we believe that Deputy Headteachers who engage with governance systems of other schools can gain a strategic, 'big-picture' outlook on leadership and school improvement.

Dissecting and rearranging our generic model, we can see that a Deputy Headteacher who aligns themselves with a governance system will be aligning with trustees and CEOs in a similar fashion to the methods suggested in this book:

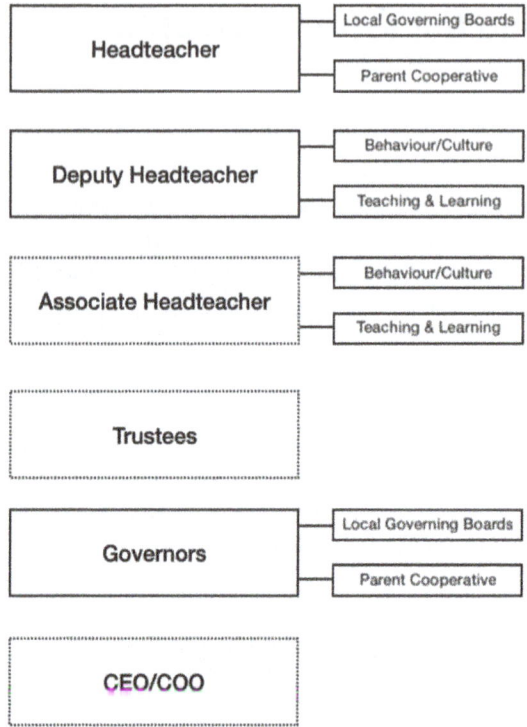

FIGURE 14: *Equality of positions of leadership*

Strategic vs operational

Often banded around as a powerful phrase, how many people actually consider the implications of an operational leader acting only strategically, bound by this enigmatic rule? Contributing to high-level decision making, you may often hear the phrase 'a critical friend' but this can have multitudinous meanings that are unhelpful. Being 'professionally curious' (EEF, 2024) is a huge asset here – and our preferred phrase – because the nature of curiosity suggests a light touch from the governor where questions can be asked and situations probed for its strengths and weaknesses. In schools, trusts and MATs where a governing body exists, there will also be roles of Vice Chair and Chair of Governors – ample space for leadership growth in a unique structure. Technically, the role of the Chair of Governors carries no significance above any other governor; they hold no more or less power. This is a point of humility for a Chair of Governors and decelerates ideas of grandeur where necessary because to be truly effective, a Chair must hold the role with humility because the reality is somewhat different. The significance of the Chair (and Vice Chair) is considerably undervalued, given too little recognition (James et al., 2012). So what is this significance and how can rising to the role of Chair help you in your own leadership journey?

Strategic thinking and governance knowledge

As Chair, your first duty is to help form a team of governors around you can help strategically guide the school – as you may have been in your setting. Long-term goals, school priorities (finance, staffing, inspection compliance) and safeguarding of the 'vision' of the school (from MAT trustees or otherwise). If you are lucky enough to be working with a governance services team, they may well be able to help you reach out to the local community for a variety of interested parties. If not, you're looking for individuals who have an interest in specific parts of school life:

- A local business person for financial insight
- Local community leaders
- Parents
- People with an interest in careers or health and safety.

From our experience, however, some of the roles (safeguarding, pupil premium, disadvantaged students, behaviour) are too important to be guessed at and individuals with current and updating educational experience are best placed to be recruited into these vital roles.

Being able to support leaders in your governance setting can help you gain an oversight of their framework of decision making and systems of accountability. Taking the time to appreciate your experience from a very different perspective could have serious and wide-ranging impacts in your setting from a growth of empathy for your own governance system to being more able to suggest school improvement opportunities that are strategically aligned and therefore likely to be taken on board.

Financial acumen

Not naturally the realm of the Deputy Headteacher, a place on a governing body can give you a unique insight into the world of school finance. Assisting with managing and allocating school budgets can help you understand the financial priorities, and constraints, of the budget that is important to help school leadership balance resources with school improvement aims. Awareness of the myriad funding challenges leadership faces and a comprehension of fiscal responsibility regarding mainstream school funding will undoubtedly increase your own cognisance of this in your setting.

Insight into different school contexts

A carefully chosen governing body will come from a variety of different backgrounds and experiences which, if used correctly, will expose you to perspectives that are outside of your own school setup and environment. A case in point: if a leader from an independent school is a governor at a mainstream academy, they will be able to witness vastly different progression, accountability structures and funding models from their own. Bringing this back to their school will allow them to empathetically suggest changes and improvements that they have witnessed in the other setting. Likewise, the independent mindset carried by the leader into the governance setting could prove advantageous when discussing solutions to strategic problems.

Perhaps most significantly, governance cultivates the ability to ask strategic questions rather than provide immediate solutions. In Deputy Headship, the expectation is often for rapid problem resolution. In governance, the responsibility centres on probing, challenging, and ensuring appropriate personnel address appropriate challenges through appropriate methodologies. This interrogative mindset proves essential for senior leadership effectiveness.

Engagement with governance opportunities is straightforward. Local authority governance teams, national recruitment databases, and professional networks provide multiple pathways for involvement. The typical time commitment ranges from ten to fifteen hours monthly, making it manageable alongside Deputy Head responsibilities while providing substantial developmental return on investment. We wholeheartedly endorse Deputy Headteachers applying to and serving in governing bodies: it brings a diverse and ever-deepening understanding of a variety of school structures, setting-specific issues and the opportunity to learn how to think strategically using a 'big picture' approach to your own leadership journey.

Aligning ambition with actions

With so many options to develop yourself, it can feel that the most efficient way of choosing your way forward is to outsource the decision to a line manager. It is not uncommon for Deputy Headteachers to find themselves sat in their performance management reviews having the inevitable conversation about starting their National Professional Qualification for Headship.

In many cases, this is the right direction of development for the individual... but not always. There are now, more than ever, many different options for Deputy Headteachers to develop their careers that do not involve headship. The crucial factor is to become clear about what your ambition is and to align that with the actions you take to develop yourself.

The growth of trusts and associated trust wide roles in areas like curriculum development, PD and behaviour means that a school senior leader with a passion for a particular area of school improvement now has the option of applying for these roles. If these kinds of roles appeal to you, consider the development that will best serve your ambition. For example, if you would like to see yourself in a leadership role around developing teaching across a group of schools, the Chartered status course (Leadership pathway) would be an excellent choice. The course deepens participants' understanding of evidence-informed practice, effective PD and improves both your leadership awareness and knowledge base around the most effective teaching practice. On the other hand, if you are motivated by the leadership of a whole organisation, look no further than a Master's degree in Educational leadership.

While these qualifications will support you in developing your own areas of interest, it is important to supplement this development with the plethora of writing from within the ecosystem of our profession. Never before has there been so many high quality books on education being written (many by people who have so generously contributed to this book). This means that the very best thinking from within the profession has never been more accessible and this is something you should certainly take advantage of.

How though, in a role that is so wonderfully yet problematically unpredictable, can a Deputy Headteacher maintain focus on their own development amidst an ever-growing list of leadership responsibilities? Programme structures vary significantly –

some requiring substantial face-to-face engagement, others offering flexible online completion. Assessment methodologies range from heavily examination-focused to practically applied. Networking opportunities differ considerably between programmes. Selection should align with both learning preferences and current professional commitments. Something that we hear a lot from school leaders is 'I just don't have the time'. This captures how school leadership *feels*. However, in reality, we do have *all* of the time. The question is how we deploy and protect it. There are times of the day when Deputy Headteachers have more control over their time than at other times. First thing in the morning is usually one example of this. So, if your development is important to you, ringfence 7 am to 8 am three times per week, securing three hours of development time on a weekly basis. Be realistic and accepting of the rhythm of the school day. During morning break, you are likely to be flooded with questions and messages that have arisen during the first part of the day and that the smooth running of the school day will require you to be attentive to these queries. Therefore, avoid ringfencing time for your own development during this time. Deputy Headship will always be a demanding and dynamic role but by viewing time as a resource that we can deploy and looking for the points in the day when you are most in control of that deployment, you can successfully match the demands of the role with your own development.

Navigating educational research

Educational research is so readily available for teachers and school leaders. The rise in research-informed practice is supported by researchers engaging with educators. More teachers and leaders are also actively collaborating with researchers to help translate the research into practice.

Recent rhetoric around the roles of education experts working outside of schools has focused on the idea that the sector would be better served with these people working in schools themselves. We do not agree. For a start, it ignores the very domain specific nature of expertise. While some people have clear expertise in navigating and illuminating educational research, that is not to say that they are experts in all areas of education. It does not mean, for example, that they are experts at teaching quadratic equations or masters of questioning techniques.

Secondly, having a group of people outside of schools themselves, working on illuminating the research for those of us inside schools means that this responsibility does not have to sit with time poor school leaders. If we embrace the full educational ecosystem, including those whose core business is outside of physical school buildings, we are likely to bring the best of what is known about how learning happens into the hands of those who need it – class teachers – much more quickly than we otherwise would be able to.

To navigate the world of educational research effectively, embrace the contributions of those outside of the day-to-day school environment.

As there is much to learn from those within the education ecosystem but outside of school buildings, you can also gain insight from research in other fields. However, it is important to be selective here. Typically, research in areas such as the medical and armed forces professions are reliable sources to consult. These are industries that rely on good leadership for success. They are also industries that have historically invested in understanding how to lead others effectively because, crudely, if these industries fail in that endeavour, people die. This also provides a useful feedback loop in that success or failure of particular approaches to leadership in these areas is quickly apparent from the fact that more people's lives are saved.

Another vital skill of the research-informed Deputy Headteacher is understanding what makes a study reliable and valid. Some indicators to look for to help form a judgement on the value of any given evidence include the following:

- Look for replicated randomised control trials. Randomised control trials ensure that two groups – intervention and control – are as close to identical as possible in expectation and therefore, any difference in outcome is likely to be due to the intervention. When these kinds of trials are replicated, they become even more reliable.

- Look for meta-analysis studies. These look at lots of research in a particular area and work out how effective something is on average. This helps to remove the contextual variance that exists in some research conclusions.

- Look for research that systematically tests alternative methods. Comparisons with alternative approaches provide excellent context.

Perhaps the most unhelpful question that school leaders can ask when they want to talk about an area of school improvement is: *'What does the research say about that?'* The problem with using research in this way is that there are always different conclusions that can be drawn from the same research and often there is valid and reliable research that concludes something entirely different to other valid and reliable research. The best Deputy Headteachers interrogate the evidence on both sides and make a judgement driven by their own context. Above all though, be prepared to explain why you have chosen a particular interpretation of the research and how your actions align with it. Otherwise, you risk falling for the latest fad of misinformation.

Context is king when it comes to applying the findings of educational research. Remember that often two applications of the same findings might look very different because they are driven by contextual differences. This is about understanding the active ingredients of the phenomenon that the research has proven – the aspects that make it work rather than the observable, often seductive, surface level features. Unfortunately, there are times when educators over focus on copying a method exactly for their school. Then in cases where teachers adapt the method, others are quick to label this as a lethal mutation (when an idea is incorrectly applied due to a lack of understanding about the active ingredients of it) when in fact it represents necessary contextual variance and the teacher may well have been making a thoughtful and necessary change. This is a warning against policing adaptations of methods too rigidly and a reminder to focus on understanding why someone has chosen a strategy.

Life outside the school building

We encourage any Deputy Headteacher to prioritise their own personal development outside of school. Whether learning a new language, travelling or taking cookery classes, having new experiences and working on projects that intrigue you will keep your school role in perspective. That is not to say that the role will feel or be any less important. Rather, it will enable you to see it in the context of the rest of your life, as one crucial part in your aim to be the version of yourself you want to be.

Maintaining this kind of perspective is difficult, especially in an environment as demanding and dynamic as school leadership. However, it will enable you to be alive to opportunities to have the kind of impact that you genuinely want to have or even just to keep options open for the future. Roles involving consultancy or coaching are attainable for school leaders with a particular interest in working with multiple schools or in helping other leaders and schools to thrive. If you think this might interest you at some point, take steps (and time) to prepare yourself for it now so that when and if the time comes, you are in a position to grab the presented opportunity.

Clare Hoods-Truman is an Executive Principle, working across schools in and around Birmingham for the Oasis trust. Clare's professional achievements have been underpinned by her excellence as a leader and her commitment to her own personal development. In the professional perspective below, she explains how important this has been to her in her career to date.

PROFESSIONAL PERSPECTIVE

By Clare Hoods-Truman – Executive Principal, Oasis Community Learning

As an Executive Principal working across diverse schools within a large Multi-Academy Trust, I have come to see self-development not as an optional extra, but as a leadership imperative. Our ability to influence others, lead with authenticity and sustain school improvement is only as strong as our commitment to our own growth.

Earlier in my career, like many leaders, I placed my development below operational demands. But experience has taught me that neglecting your own progression ultimately limits your impact. Some of my most effective leadership decisions have emerged from purposeful investment in my own development – whether that's been through academic study, coaching, engaging with sector-wide governance, or accessing thought leadership beyond education.

> The reality is: leadership roles are demanding and complex. To navigate them well, you must protect space for reflection, strategic thinking, and re-energising. High-quality professional development; especially when aligned with your values and long-term goals, can transform not only your practice, but the culture you shape for others.
>
> Equally, developing yourself isn't just about formal qualifications. Immersing yourself in research, connecting across networks, reading widely and even exploring interests outside education all contribute to a grounded, resilient and perspective-rich leadership style. These moments outside school can help recalibrate your sense of purpose and unlock renewed clarity.
>
> My advice is simple: don't outsource your development. Be deliberate. Be strategic. Know your 'why' and align your growth to it. When you invest in your own learning, you model that culture for your team and you strengthen your ability to lead in ways that are not only effective but enduring.

Developing yourself may be a task that often fails to become a priority as it acquiesces to the multitudinous nature of our job. Keeping on top of your personal development – above and beyond that of the prescribed PD in your setting – can be a huge and insurmountable undertaking.

9

Conclusion: bridging the gap

The role of Deputy Head, as we have found, is one of such rich complexity that to summarise the methods of '*Succeeding as ...*' is to reduce the intricacies of the job to the point that we minimise its importance. Far-reaching and multi-faceted, being a Deputy Head is more than being a professional stand–in for the Headteacher, but is a role that ranges from dedicated areas of school improvement (behaviour or teaching and learning), associate roles for PD and staff training, balancing teaching timetables and – when required – deputising for the Headteacher.

No two Deputy Heads are alike. Job descriptions vary and we can all speak to dramatically different experiences, whether that is the job itself, our Headteachers past and present or our colleagues and students. We have taken the time to speak to, and receive advice and contributions from, a wide variety of voices in education from serving Deputy Heads to those who have made the move to higher leadership and from those in executive leadership who know the value of a leader succeeding as a Deputy Head; the result of which now rests in your hands.

We have explored the paradoxes that define Deputy Headship – those moments when you need to be simultaneously supportive and challenging, strategic and operational, authentic and adaptive. If you feel that these contradictions are impossible to navigate, you aren't alone. Every successful Deputy Head has stood where you're standing now, wondering how on earth they are supposed to balance these competing demands.

Core themes

There is no perfect formula for navigating these challenges. However, there is a way of thinking about your role that can guide you through even the most complex situations. This thinking is built around the core themes that have emerged throughout our exploration.

Leadership alignment

Whether you're aligning with your Headteacher, governing body or members of your SLT/SMT, sharing a common vision and values with these key stakeholders is vital in your success. Sometimes, this will involve compromising on your part for the benefit of the greater good. Such assimilation in a setting can, for a short period of time, ensure professional transactions occur in a manner that is positive for the whole. Compromise is, however, never something in which to settle and a successful Deputy Head will flourish at a setting and with other leaders to whom they can fully align.

When facing any leadership decision, this alignment becomes your compass. Does this align with your Headteacher's vision? If not, how can you influence positively? Does this serve our students' needs? If the answer here is no, then regardless of any other pressures or considerations, you need to stop and reassess. Your ultimate accountability is to the young people in your care, and that principle should be unwavering even when everything else feels uncertain.

Relationship management and trust building

Your ability to successfully manage the myriad relationships at a school setting is significant. As a Deputy Head, you are the bridge between the Headteacher, staff, students, parents and the wider community. This natural positioning requires managing these relationships across different levels to ensure smooth communication and implementation of policies that affect all of them in some way. Doing this effectively can foster a collaborative environment where staff feel valued and supported, leading to higher morale and better teamwork.

Trust is fundamental to leadership and when staff and students trust their Deputy Head, they are more likely to follow guidance or feel comfortable voicing their concerns and suggestions. Trusting you can help resolve conflicts more effectively and when people trust your intentions and judgement, they are more willing to engage in constructive dialogue and find solutions.

This trust building requires constant attention to the relational impact of your decisions. Will this build or damage relationships? Every decision you make as a Deputy Head has relational consequences. Sometimes you will be required to make decisions that are temporarily uncomfortable for relationships in service of longer-term goals. But if you're consistently damaging the relationships that underpin your effectiveness, you undermine your own ability to lead.

The development of staff and self

PD is, and may always be, the single greatest lever of change. As a force of that change, developing those around you is a responsibility that, again, requires balancing research evidence with the unique needs of your school environment. Similarly, support staff – often overlooked in sweeping developmental initiatives – require intentional support and opportunities for growth within their roles.

A successful Deputy Head must do their best to ensure all members of the wider school family feel valued and have access to the appropriate support for both their professional and personal development. The role also includes developing other leaders, which involves navigating the complexities of ambition, preparedness, and enthusiasm. Supporting aspiring leaders without overwhelming them and encouraging reluctant leaders requires careful timing and strategic conversation and is wholly dependent on sacrifices of time and organisation made by the Deputy Head.

This development focus extends to yourself as well. The most effective Deputy Heads we know cultivate a development mindset – approaching every challenge as an opportunity for growth. What can you learn from this situation? How can you help others grow through it? What would you do differently if faced with something similar in the future? This mindset transforms the inevitable mistakes and setbacks from sources of frustration into stepping stones for improvement.

The challenges of the Deputy Headteacher are framed throughout as challenges and while we suggest practical and theoretical solutions, these are also underpinned by, we hope, a tangible sense of three guiding principles:

- Decency
- Humility
- Authenticity.

These principles form what we think of as your decency test – a way of ensuring that even in the most pressured moments, you're acting with integrity. When faced with difficult situations, challenging conversations, quick fixes that impact negatively on others and the kinds of decisions that you are paid the big bucks – perhaps one day – to make, ask yourself: have you faced every conversation acknowledging that there is a person on the other side of it? Have you protected their dignity and their agency throughout? Are you treating this person as you would want to be treated? Are you being honest about your motivations, both with others and with yourself?

When looking to implement change that you know is likely to be unsettling or challenging for others, have you led the way with authenticity, avoiding the temptation to be something that you are not? This doesn't mean you can't adapt your approach – in fact, the best leaders are constantly adapting. But adaptation should enhance your authentic self, not contradict it. If you find yourself consistently acting in ways that feel fundamentally wrong to you, then either the situation needs to change or you need to reassess whether this is the right role for you.

People follow leaders who are authentically true to themselves, so it's important to remain authentic. As a Deputy Head there will be times when you don't have all the answers or a clear direction. In those moments, can you embrace humility and vulnerability? Bridging the paradox to reveal vulnerability as a strength and remaining true to your core principles will help underpin your success as a Deputy Headteacher.

Deputy Headteachers, and other educational leadership roles, face unique challenges in managing both strategic thinking for long-term success and daily operational demands. The temptation to dive in as the key problem solver in the daily running of the school has the potential to detract from the critical and reflective thinking necessary for long-term development; it's in the balancing of these responsibilities that you find the essential time for fostering personal and context-dependent growth.

If you find yourself in a smaller team, effective whole-school leadership necessitates collaboration and genuine buy-in from the team around you which should, perhaps, come from a more inclusive discovery of change process. Shane Leaning, an expert in organisational change and coaching, speaks about there being no need for team 'buy-in' if members of the school community have played a significant and meaningful part in the change being proposed (EduPulse, 2024). Sustainable change is driven by the shared beliefs and shared language in effective practices as opposed to mere compliance. If Deputy Headteachers commit to evidence-informed patient approaches, fostering collaborative and imperative environments, they can lead impactful and enduring change.

Your first 90 days as Deputy Headteacher: a plan to turn insight into action

Days 1–30 Listen, learn and build trust

Goals:

- Start building relationships across the school community.
- Understand the school culture, systems, and routines.
- Establish visibility and approachability.

Actions:

- Hold one-to-one or small group meetings with the Headteacher, staff, pupils (e.g. school council), and parents (PTA).
- Review key documents: SDP, Ofsted reports, safeguarding, curriculum frameworks.

- Visit lessons across year groups and observe routines.
- Attend assemblies, staff briefings and team meetings.
- Familiarise yourself with data and pastoral systems.
- Start a reflection log to track insights and questions.

Days 31–60 Assess and align with your team

Goals:

- Identify areas for early impact.
- Align priorities with Headteacher and SLT.
- Start contributing strategically.

Actions:

- Analyse pupil progress, attendance, behaviour and staff wellbeing data.
- Take ownership of agreed responsibilities (e.g. behaviour, curriculum, PD).
- Conduct informal audits: learning walks, book looks, pupil voice.
- Clarify expectations and define your leadership role.
- Co-lead a staff meeting or PD session.
- Begin offering informal staff support or mentoring.

Days 61–90 Lead with impact

Goals:

- Launch early initiatives.
- Demonstrate visible and purposeful leadership.
- Reflect on impact and adapt.

Actions:

- Roll out an initial improvement project (e.g. feedback policy, coaching model).
- Share progress and reflections with SLT and staff.
- Monitor and evaluate early impact using data and feedback.
- Lead a second PD session.
- Collect feedback from staff and adjust plans as needed.
- Finalise and share your refined leadership focus areas.

Questions for you to revisit each term:

- What are your priority areas?
- Who are your key stakeholders?
- What immediate questions do you have for your Headteacher?
- PD ideas that you have already tried and would like to implement?

Pace yourself and acknowledge your efforts

If you feel overwhelmed by the scope of what we've covered in this book, remember that leadership development is a marathon, not a sprint. Rather than trying to implement everything at once, choose one area to focus on over the next three months. Spend time observing and assessing your current approach. What's working well? What feels awkward or ineffective? Where do you see the biggest opportunity for improvement? Then implement one new strategy from this book, gather feedback about how this change lands, and refine your approach based on what you've learned. Deputy Headship isn't about perfection. It's about continuous improvement, authentic relationships, and serving your school community with decency and professionalism. You will make mistakes – we all do. What matters is how you learn from them and how you use those lessons to become a better leader.

The role of Deputy Head is demanding, complex and sometimes thankless. But it is also one of the most rewarding positions in education. You have the opportunity to shape the daily experience of hundreds of young people and dozens of colleagues. You can create the conditions for others to flourish and succeed. You can bridge the gap between vision and reality; between strategy and implementation; between the individual and the system. That is a privilege and a responsibility that deserves to be taken seriously and we hope that this book has given you the tools to help you succeed in that vital work.

PAGES FOR YOUR PERSONAL REFLECTION NOTES

CONCLUSION: BRIDGING THE GAP

A note from the authors

Adam

I hope that you have enjoyed reading this book and that you have taken a great deal from it from it to help you in your leadership journey. Being a successful Deputy Head is no mean feat: it requires perhaps the most varied skill set in a school because the responsibilities that drive your role have the potential to change at a moment's notice. To reduce the messages from this book into a single paragraph is simply not possible but to leave you with what I see as the essence of Deputy Headship, I urge you to focus on knowing yourself, knowing your stuff and knowing your people. Leading authentically is only possible if you know who the authentic *you* is. You need to know your strengths, your weaknesses, your character strengths and flaws so well that you can deliberately lead with the part of you that is most useful to the situation. You must also know your stuff: charisma – if you are lucky enough to have it! – will get people enthused, but motivation will not sustain when the gaps in your knowledge become apparent and problematic. To be a credible Deputy Head, your knowledge of key areas of school life – the areas we have written about – need to be sufficient to inspire trust and faith in those that follow you. Of course, you do not need to know everything and it is perhaps most important that you know the areas where you do lack knowledge so that you can seek out people who can fill in the gaps. Finally: know your people. People are at the heart of every leadership interaction and decision that you make. They are people first and professionals second and you need to know *who* people are in order to create the conditions for them to thrive.

The role of the Deputy Head is challenging but this only increases the rewarding nature of the role. The influence you hold over the daily lives and the development of those you lead is a responsibility that is undoubtedly a privilege. Above all else, the impact you stand to have, through your leadership, over the lives of the students in your school is the beacon of inspiration that connects you to that central privilege of the position you hold and will keep you on track to succeed as a Deputy Head.

Chris

Being a Deputy Headteacher is, in the rapidly changing world of education, a challenging and conflicting role, not least because it is becoming increasingly hard to define. School systems, funding and regulatory bodies are in a constant state of flux and, as such, the role of a Deputy Headteacher becomes as fluid and flexible as the school contexts in which they serve. Like attempting to pin a cloud to a display board, we have tried to select areas of common struggle and success that can help anyone understand the broad nature of the role as well as those who wish to succeed in it.

Teaching is one of the most important and exceptional jobs there is and, therefore, to be in any way associated with leading it is the greatest of privileges. This book is written with you in mind: you the inspiring leader, you the new and current Deputy Head and you the educational leader looking for a moment of inspiration from our professional and wonderfully varied perspectives.

Understanding that an empathetic and sensitive Deputy Headteacher can fundamentally improve and change an entire school context for the better is perhaps the most important lesson we hope you can take from this book. We will all fail if we do not succeed in lifting each other up to celebrate our gains and wins as well as coming together in solidarity during moments of struggle and loss. Succeeding as a Deputy Head is about knowing yourself and knowing how that strength can empower others to carry the torch of educational leadership for the betterment of those that matter the most: our students.

We leave our closing remarks to Joanna, who is an aspiring Deputy Head:

PROFESSIONAL PERSPECTIVE

By Joanna Tompkins – Associate Assistant Head and Head of Creative Industries at a Secondary School in Birmingham

Succeeding as a Deputy Head has arrived at exactly the right time in my career and progression. I had been searching for a tool which was informative, meaningful and reflective and *Succeeding as a Deputy Head* is a book which has become essential for me as a manual to which I return daily to reflect on my practice. Reading this book has reinforced my want to develop my career as a Deputy Headteacher.

I have felt an overwhelming sense of kismet and kinship with the people who have shared their stories and advice. Ever since I was lucky enough to read Gwyn Ap Harri's story speaking to the fragility of leadership, I felt as though I had the permission to reflect on my own

> experiences in the profession and reminded me that, as professionals, no experience we have is singular. The model of 'trust me.../show me...' has been crucial in helping to construct the culture that I am aiming to build within my leadership practice.
>
> As I take on leading more Teaching and Learning responsibility at my academy, using the reflection tools in this book, particularly in 'Leading whole school areas' has encouraged a permanent state of reflective practice. I have found myself searching back to reflection tasks after I have led whole school training to identify my own areas of development as an emerging leader.
>
> There truly is something for every emerging leader in this book to further their development. From identifying 'hidden leaders', which is something I have begun to identify using the 'commonalities of good leadership' model, to 'Building Trust and Setting Standards' in a school which has suffered periods of fractured routines and foundations.
>
> From emerging leaders everywhere, thank you; we needed this.

The role of the Deputy Headteacher is multifaceted and fraught with paradoxes and challenges that all require a delicate balance between personal convictions and professional responsibilities. By embracing these challenges with strategic thinking, Deputy Headteachers can drive meaningful and lasting change. They do this by intentionally cultivating supportive relationships and committing to evidence-informed practices. When done well, this leadership results in happy and successful young people who are taught by professionally curious and educationally ethical teachers.

References

Ausubel, D.P. (2000) *The Acquisition and Retention of Knowledge: A Cognitive View*. New York: Springer Science and Business Media.

Bambrick-Santoyo, P. (2016) *Get Better Faster: A 90-day Plan for Coaching New Teachers*. San Francisco: Jossey-Bass.

Brené Brown, C. (2018) *Dare to Lead: Brave Work. Tough Conversations. Whole Hearts*. London: Vermilion.

Bruni, L. and Tufano, F. (2017) 'The value of vulnerability: The transformative capacity of risky trust'. *Judgment and Decision Making*, 12(4), pp. 408–414. Available at: https://doi.org/10.1017/S1930297500006276 [Accessed 3 June 2025].

Callaghan, J. (1976) A rational debate on the facts. Available online at: www.educationengland.org.uk/documents/speeches/1976ruskin.html (Accessed July 25, 2025).

Cherniss, C. (2010) 'Emotional intelligence: Toward clarification of a concept'. *Industrial and Organizational Psychology*, 3(2), pp. 110–126.

Clapham, A. (2024) 'Undiminishing school governance: investigating 'governance maturity theory' for school governing bodies'. *Journal of Education Policy*, 39(6), pp. 899–918. Available at: https://doi.org/10.1080/02680939.2024.2337031 [Accessed 3 June 2025].

Clay, B. (2017) 'CPD for school support staff'. *SecEd*, 1 November. Available at: https://www.sec-ed.co.uk/content/best-practice/cpd-for-school-support-staff/ [Accessed 3 June 2025].

Coates, S. (2012) *Headstrong*. England: John Catt.

Coe, R. (2023) 'Why are we holding out for more professional development time (even though school leaders say they can't manage it)?'. *Evidence Based Education*, 19 July. Available at: https://evidencebased.education/

why-are-we-holding-out-for-more-professional-development-time-even-though-school-leaders-say-they-cant-manage-it/ [Accessed 3 June 2025].

Cottingham, S. (2023) *Ausubel's Meaningful Learning in Action*. Suffolk: John Catt.

Cottinghatt, S. (2024) 'Cognitive coaching: changing minds and changing practice'. *Substack*. Available at: https://cognitivecoaching.substack.com/p/cognitive-coaching-changing-minds [Accessed 3 June 2025].

Covey, S. R. (1989) *The 7 habits of highly effective people: Restoring the character ethic*. New York: Free Press.

Deans for Impact (2016) *Practice with Purpose: The Emerging Science of Expertise*. Austin, TX: Deans for Impact.

Development Dimensions International. (2023). *Leadership Trends for 2024: The Year of Trust*. Retrieved from DDI blog ddiworld.comddiworld.com.

Development Dimensions International. (2023). *7 Ways Leaders Build Trust in the Workplace*. Retrieved from DDI blogDrucker, P.F. (1991) 'The new productivity challenge'. *Harvard Business Review*, 3(3). Available at: https://doi.org/10.4236/ce.2013.45048 [Accessed 3 June 2025].

Earley, P. and Weindling, D. (2004) Understanding School Leadership (Published in association with the British Educational Leadership and Management Society) Ebbinghaus, H. (1885) *Über das Gedächtnis*. Leipzig: Dunker.

Edmondson, A. (1999) 'Psychological safety and learning behaviour in work teams'. *Administrative Science Quarterly*, 44(2), pp. 350–383.

Edmondson, A.C. (2012) *Teaming: How Organizations Learn, Innovate, and Compete in the Knowledge Economy*. Hoboken, NJ: John Wiley & Sons.

Education Reform Act of 1988, 32 Stat. 172, 20 U.S.C. 3401 (1988).

EduPulse Podcast (2024) 'Organisational Change: In Conversation with Shane Leaning'. *EduPulse*, October 2024. Available at: https://open.spotify.com/episode/6mwOQUPejILAsCWGCl1oTM?si=CTV4hIYiROqmhNDE_XC6LQ [Accessed 3 June 2025].

EEF (2021) 'Improving behaviour in schools'. *Education Endowment Foundation*, 27 October. Available at: https://educationendowmentfoundation.org.uk/education-evidence/guidance-reports/behaviour [Accessed 3 June 2025].

EEF (2024) *The EEF Guide to the Pupil Premium (Updated)*. London: Education Endowment Foundation.

Emira, M. (2013) 'Support staff leadership: Opportunities and challenges'. *Leadership*, 9(1), pp. 23–41. Available at: https://doi.org/10.1177/1742715012455128 [Accessed 3 June 2025].

Farndon, S. (2019) 'What is instructional coaching?'. *Ambition Institute*. Available at: https://www.ambition.org.uk/blog/what-instructional-coaching/ [Accessed 3 June 2025].

Fourmy, R. (2023) 'Why executives need to practice vulnerable leadership - and how to do it'. *DDI World*, 24 August. Available at: https://www.ddiworld.com/blog/vulnerable-leadership [Accessed 3 June 2025].

Fullan, M. (2007) *Leading in a Culture of Change: Personal Action Guide and Workbook*. San Francisco: Jossey-Bass.

Goodrich, J. (2024) Responsive coaching: *Evidence informed Instructional coaching that works for every teacher in your school*. England: John Catt.

Goffee, R. and Jones, G. (2019) *Why Should Anyone Be Led by You?: What It Takes to Be an Authentic Leader*. Boston: Harvard Business Press.

Goleman, D. (2000) 'Leadership that gets results'. *Harvard Business Review*, pp. 78–90.

Goleman, D. (2009) *Working with Emotional Intelligence*. London: Bloomsbury.

Hall, E.T. (1976) *Beyond Culture*. New York: Anchor Books.

Hart, N. (2022) *Creating a Strong Culture and Positive Climate in Schools: Building Knowledge to Bring About Improvement*. Abingdon: Taylor & Francis.

Harvard Business Review (2022)

Hattie, J. (2009) *Visible Learning: A Synthesis of Over 800 Meta-Analyses Relating to Achievement*. Abingdon: Routledge.

Hempson, K. (2014) 'Reluctant leaders and autonomous followers: Leadership tactics in professional service firms'. Available at: https://www.bayes.city.ac.uk/__data/assets/pdf_file/0018/222723/Reluctant-Leaders-EMPSON.pdf?bustCache=46494072%2F%2F&mod=article_inline [Accessed 3 June 2025].

Herzberg, F.I. (1968) 'One more time: How do you motivate employees?'. *Harvard Business Review*, 46(1), pp. 53–62.

Hoffman, B.J., Woehr, D.J., Maldagen-Youngjohn, R. and Lyons, B.D. (2011) 'Great man or great myth? A quantitative review of the relationship between individual differences and leader effectiveness'. *Journal of Occupational and Organizational Psychology*, 84(2). Available at: https://doi.org/10.1348/096317909X485207 [Accessed 3 June 2025].

Ireland, P. and Pattinson, N. (2021) 'Module 7031CRB, Leadership Theory'. *Coventry: FutureLearn*, Coventry University. Available at: https://www.futurelearn.com/courses/origins-of-leadership/1/steps/1130540 [Accessed 3 June 2025].

James, C., Jones, J., Connolly, M., Brammer, S., Fertig, M. and James, J. (2012) 'The role of the chair of the school governing body in England'. *School Leadership & Management*, 32(1), pp. 3–19. Available at: https://doi.org/10.1080/13632434.2011.642356 [Accessed 3 June 2025].

Jopling, M. and Zimmermann, D. (2023) 'Exploring vulnerability from teachers' and young people's perspectives in school contexts in England and Germany'. *Research Papers in Education*, 38(5), pp. 828–845. Available at: https://doi.org/10.1080/02671522.2023.2179656 [Accessed 3 June 2025].

Kahneman, D. (2012) *Thinking, Fast and Slow*. London: Penguin.

Kennedy, M., (2016) 'Parsing the practice of teaching'. *Journal of Teacher Education* 67, 6–17.

King, B.J., n.d. For me, losing a tennis match isn't failure, it's research. [online] Available at: https://www.azquotes.com/quote/556572 [Accessed 11 June 2025].

Kleynhans, D.J., Heyns, M.M., Stander, M.W. and de Beer, L.T. (2022) 'Authentic Leadership, Trust (in the Leader), and Flourishing: Does Precariousness Matter?'. *Frontiers in*

Psychology, 13, 798759. Available at: https://doi.org/10.3389/fpsyg.2022.798759 [Accessed 3 June 2025].

Knight, B., Turner, D. and Dekkers, J. (2013) 'The future of the practicum: Addressing the knowing-doing gap'. In: *Teacher Education in Australia: Investigations into Programming, Practicum and Partnership*, pp. 63–76.

Kohlbeck, A. (2024) 'Reframing post-lesson assessment and feedback: A case study'. *Impact*. The Chartered College of Teaching.

Kotter, J. (1996) *Leading Change*. Boston: Harvard Business School Press.

Kraft, M.A. and Papay, J.P. (2014) 'Can professional environments in schools promote teacher development? Explaining heterogeneity in returns to teaching experience'. *Educational Evaluation and Policy Analysis*.

Lam, L.W. and Lau, D.C. (2012) 'Feeling lonely at work: Investigating the consequences of unsatisfactory workplace relationships'. *The International Journal of Human Resource Management*, 23(20), pp. 4265–4282. Available at: https://doi.org/10.1080/09585192.2012.665070 [Accessed 3 June 2025].

Lehman, D.W., O'Connor, K., Kovács, B. and Newman, G.E. (2019) 'Authenticity'. *Academy of Management Annals*, 13, pp. 1–42. Available at: https://doi.org/10.5465/annals.2017.0047 [Accessed 3 June 2025].

Lemov, D. (2010) Teach like a champion: 49 techniques that put students on the path to college (K-12). New York: Jossey-Bass.

Lewis, J., Outhwaite, D., Tupling, C., Gibson, M. and Ferri, G. (2023) 'The Changing Role of the Headteacher in England Post Academisation'. *British Education Studies Association*. ISSN: 17582199.

Male, T. and Wright, N. (2015) 'Taking over the Controls: A Case Study of Headteacher Internship in England'. Available at: https://doi.org/10.13140/RG.2.1.2150.6003 [Accessed 3 June 2025].

Marquet, D. (2013) *Turn the Ship Around!: A True Story of Building Leaders by Breaking the Rules*. Portfolio Penguin.

McVey, T. (2020) 'Why consistency is key'. *Impact*, Part of My College, 9. Available at: https://my.chartered.college/impact_article/why-consistency-is-key/ [Accessed 3 June 2025].

Mercer, D. (1996) 'Can They Walk on Water?: Professional isolation and the secondary headteacher'. *School Organisation*, 16(2), pp. 165–178. Available at: https://doi.org/10.1080/02601369650037967 [Accessed 3 June 2025].

Miao, C., Humphrey, R.H. and Qian, S. (2018) 'Emotional intelligence and authentic leadership: A meta-analysis'. *Leadership & Organization Development Journal*, 39(5), pp. 679–690.

Michaela Community School (2024) 'Ethos and values'. *Michaela Community School*. Available at: https://michaela.education/home/secondary-school-wembley/ethos-values-michaela-community-school-wembley/ [Accessed 3 June 2025].

Miller, P. (2018) *The Nature of School Leadership, Global Practice Perspectives*. London: Palgrave Macmillan.

Northouse, P.G. (2018) *Leadership: Theory and Practice* (8th ed.). Thousand Oaks, CA: SAGE Publications.

OECD (2010) *PISA 2009 Results: What Makes a School Successful? Resources, Policies and Practices Vol IV*. Paris: Organisation for Economic Co-operation and Development.

Omadeke, J. (2022) 'The best leaders aren't afraid to be vulnerable'. *Harvard Business Review*. Available at: https://hbr.org/2022/07/the-best-leaders-arent-afraid-of-being-vulnerable [Accessed 3 June 2025].

Passey, C. (2024) 'Meaningful Leadership'. *EduPulse*. Available at: https://www.edupulse.co/post/meaningful-leadership-blog [Accessed 3 June 2025].

Passey, C. (2025) 'Integrating Vulnerability and Reflective Practices in Educational Leadership: A Framework for Professional Growth'. *Impact*. The Chartered College of Teaching.

Percival, A. in Sealy, C. (2020) *The researchED Guide to The Curriculum: An Evidence-Informed Guide for Teachers*. Suffolk: John Catt.

Peregrym, D. and Wollf, R. (2013) 'Values-based leadership: The foundation of transformational servant leadership'. *Journal of Values-Based Leadership*, 6(2), pp. 1–14.

Rogers, C. (1954) 'Toward a Theory of Creativity'. *ETC: A Review of General Semantics*.

Rosenshine, B. and Stevens, R. (1986) 'Teaching functions'. In: Wittrock, M.C. (ed.) *Handbook of Research on Teaching* (3rd ed.), pp. 376–391. New York: Macmillan.

Schein, E.H. (2010) *Organisational Culture & Leadership* (4th ed.). San Francisco: Jossey-Bass.

Schaffner (2024)

Sherrington, T. (2019) *Rosenshine's Principles in Action*. Suffolk: John Catt.

Sherrington, T. (2024) 'A Behaviour Perspective'. *Teacherhead*. Available at: https://teacherhead.com/2024/04/02/a-behaviour-perspective/ [Accessed 3 June 2025].

Sims, S. (2017) 'TALIS 2013: Working conditions, teacher job satisfaction and retention'. *DfE Working Paper*.

Sims, S., Fletcher-Wood, H., O'Mara-Eves, A., Cottingham, S., Goodrich, J., Van Herwegen, J. and Anders, J. (2022) 'Effective teacher professional development: new theory and a meta-analytic test? (CEPEO Working Paper No. 22-02)'. *Centre for Education Policy and Equalising Opportunities*, UCL. Available at: https://EconPapers.repec.org/RePEc:ucl:cepeow:22-02 [Accessed 3 June 2025].

Sims, S., Fletcher-Wood, H., O'Mara-Eves, A., Cottingham, S., Stansfield, C., Van Herwegen, J. and Andres, J. (2021) 'Review Identifying the characteristics of more effective professional development'. *Education Endowment Foundation*. Available at: https://educationendowmentfoundation.org.uk/education-evidence/evidence-reviews/teacher-professional-development-characteristics [Accessed 3 June 2025].

Sims, S., Moss, G., & Marshall, E. (2021) *Effective teacher professional development: Evidence review*. Education Endowment Foundation. (Available at: https://educationendowmentfoundation.org.uk)

Skip, A. and Hopwood, V. (2019) 'Deployment of Teaching Assistants in schools'. *Department for Education*, June. Available at: https://assets.publishing.service.gov.uk/media/5d1397fc40f0b6350e1ab56b/Deployment_of_teaching_assistants_report.pdf [Accessed 3 June 2025].

Smart, P., Mott, D., Sycara, K., Braines, D., Strub, M. and Shadbolt, N. (2009) 'Shared Understanding within Military Coalitions: A Definition and Review of Research Challenges'. *The International Journal of Human-Computer Studies.*

Strictland, S. (2023) *They don't behave for me.* England: John Catt.

Teasley, M.L. (2016) 'Organizational Culture and Schools: A Call for Leadership and Collaboration'. *Children & Schools*, 39(1), pp. 3–6. Available at: https://doi.org/10.1093/cs/cdw048 [Accessed 3 June 2025].

Thomas, M. (2018) 'The Nature and Nurture of Education'. *Centre for Educational Neuroscience*. Available at: http://www.educationalneuroscience.org.uk/2018/07/13/the-nature-and-nurture-of-education/ [Accessed 3 June 2025].

Trent, R.J. (2004) 'Team leadership at the 100-foot level'. *Team Performance Management*, 10(5/6), pp. 94–103. Available at: https://doi.org/10.1108/13527590410556818 [Accessed 3 June 2025].

Van de Brande, J. and Zuccollo, J. (2021) 'The effects of high-quality professional development on teachers and students: A cost-benefit analysis'. *Education Policy Institute*. Available at: https://epi.org.uk/wp-content/uploads/2021/04/EPI-CPD-entitlement-cost-benefit-analysis.2021.pdf [Accessed 3 June 2025].

Waters, M. (2022) *A Curious Curriculum: Teaching Foundation Subjects Well.* Crown House Publishing.

Wiliam, D. (2018) *Creating the Schools Our Children Need: Why What We're Doing Now Won't Help Much (And What We Can Do Instead).* Learning Sciences International.

Willingham, D.T. (2010) *Why Don't Students Like School?: A Cognitive Scientist Answers Questions About How the Mind Works and What It Means for the Classroom* San Francisco: Jossey-Bass.

Index

Abbiss, Hannah 37–9
accountability 81, 82, 158, 162, 167, 204
   outcome-driven approach 150–1
   process-driven approach 151
   psychological safety vs. 148–9, 151
   shared 152, 153–4, 167
   for teacher development 147–54
active listening 48, 51, 172
Alexander, Sally 4, 6–7
ambitious leaders 14, 184
   collaboration 187
   innovation 187
   leadership opportunities 184–6
Ap Harri, Gwyn 14–17, 24, 33, 82
Ausubel, David 88
authenticity 41–2, 217
authentic leadership 31, 40–4, 52–6

Bambrick-Santoyo, P. 161
behaviour, leadership of 99–100, 109–10
   circle of influence 102, 106–7
   collaborative cultural design 108–9
   key context of school 100–1
Brown, Brené 68

capacity, concept of 30, 31, 33
Chair of Governors 203–5
circle of control 86–7, 88
circle of influence 86–7, 111
circle of no control 87, 88, 94
Clay, Bridget 128
coaching 83–5, 90–5, 111
   instructional 160–6
Coe, Rob 128, 132
collaboration 81–2, 111, 132, 187, 217–18
   between Deputy Headteacher and Headteacher 24–5
communication 6–7, 106, 188
   active listening 48, 51, 172
   constructive communication techniques 51
   conversation starters 25, 49
   with Headteacher 19, 20, 23, 25
   open 20, 23, 45, 48, 52
   with staff 22
   with support staff 126–7
complementary understanding 26
confident leaders 171
consistency, standards 58, 68, 69–70
Cottinghatt, Sarah 171
curriculum leadership 87

autonomy for designing key concepts, delegation 89–90
coaching and mentoring 90–5
control and influence 88
development timelines 98
generalised knowledge 88
key concepts 88
pre-mortem process 99
strategies 98–9
structured feedback 98

Dare to Lead (Brown) 68
Deans for Impact 83
delegation 59, 64–7, 79–80
circle of influence 86–7
coaching and mentoring 83–5
collaboration 81–2
considerations for 85–7
culture 82–3
decision-making delays 80
deliberate practice for 83–4
of designing key concepts in curriculum leadership 89–90
key guiding principles 82
Deputy Headteacher
first 90 days as 218–20
goals of 12
responsibilities 3, 13, 57
title, meaning of 13–14
Deputy Headteacher
professional development 191–200
career development 196–7, 206
as Chair of Governors 203–5
equality of positions of 202
financial acumen 204
governance knowledge 203–4
governance opportunities 201–2, 205
headship, assumption of 201
motivation 196
personal ambition with chosen development path, aligning 205–7
personal development 210–12
post-nominals of 196–7, 206
strategic thinking 203–4
strategic *vs.* operational 202–5, 217
using educational research 207–10
Drucker, Peter 109

Earley, P. 150
Ebbinghaus, Hermann 131
Edmondson, Amy 139, 148
educational accountability 150
Education Reform Act (1988) 150
effective teacher professional development programmes 156–60
emotional intelligence (EI) 30–4, 37, 42, 54
emotional quotient 31, 32

Fullan, M. 192

generalised knowledge 88
Gibbs, Sam 74, 75–7, 198
Goffee, R. 40, 54
Goleman, D. 31, 37
Goodrich, Josh 162; 163–6

INDEX

Hall, E.T. 82
Hart, Nick 28
Hattie, John 155
Heads of Schools 12
Headteacher
  changing role of 12
  as Deputy Headteacher 19
  hope *vs.* trust on Deputy
    Head 15–16, 18–19
  leadership 19, 28
  responsibilities of 13
Headteacher, aligning with
  11, 214
  arguments and
    disagreements between
    Deputy Head and 21, 23,
    28–9
  best practices for successful
    relationship 20, 21, 22,
    23, 24
  collaboration between
    Deputy Headteacher
    and 24–5
  conversation starters 25
  critical engagement 21–2
  cultural alignment 28–30
  dysfunctional relationship,
    red flags of 21, 22, 23,
    24–5
  emotional intelligence
    30–4, 42
  honest conversations 20, 23
  leadership 19
  negative conflict/
    misalignment 28–9
  shared understanding 25–8
  staff advocacy 22
  supportive alignment 20–1
  trust, maintaining 23–4
  vision, goals and decisions 20

Herzberg, F.I. 125
Hoffman, B.J. 36, 37
Hoods-Truman, Clare 211–12
hope 15, 18–19, 82
Hopwood, V. 126

identical understanding 26
inspirational leaders 173
instructional coaching 160–1
  implementation challenges
    161–2
  school cultural impact on 162
Ireland, P. 29

Jones, G. 40, 54

Knight, B. 160
knowing-doing gap 159
knowledge 88, 96–7
Kotter, John 65, 119
Kraft, M.A. 83

leaders and leadership 31, 169,
  189–90
  ambitious 14, 184–90
  attributes of 170
  authentic 31, 40–4, 52–6, 217
  collaboration 187
  confident and assured 171
  definition 169
  delegation *see* delegation
  emotional intelligence 31, 37
  Headteacher 19, 28
  innovation 187
  as innovative thinker 171–2
  inspirational 173
  leading by example 187–8
  models, generic hierarchy
    of 13
  nurturing 175–7
  opportunities 184–6

INDEX

reluctant 177–8, 216
styles 69
theory 35–40
traits 36
values-based 67–9
vulnerability 60–2
Leading Change (Kotter) 119
Lehman, D.W. 41, 42
Lewis, J. 12
Lloyd, Swabra 199–200
Local Governing Body (LGB) 12

Male, T. 19
market accountability 150
Marquet, David 79, 90, 110
mental models 84, 146, 147, 172
mentoring 83–5, 90–5, 111
Miao, C. 31
middle leaders and leadership 59, 66, 80, 84, 88, 189
Milne, Stuart 4, 5
moral accountability 150
Multi-Academy Trusts (MATs) 12

non-defensive communication 51
Northouse, P.G. 169

Omadeke, J. 60
open communication 20, 23, 45, 48, 52
organisational culture 28–30, 82–3, 137
outcome-driven accountability 150–1

Papay, J.P. 83
Passey, Attiye 135–6
Passey, C. 60
Passey, Shaun 33
Pattinson, N. 29

Percival, Andrew 88, 96–8
Peregrym, D. 67
personal development, leadership of 102–5
power imbalances, strategies for managing 44–55
pre-mortem process 99
problem solving strategies
  authenticity, finding strength in 52–5
  compromising 50, 214
  conflict resolution 47–8, 50, 51–2
  environment for open communication, creating 48
  following up and reflection on conflict resolution process 51–2
  misunderstandings, clarifying 48–9
  remaining patient and resilient 47
  right time and place for crucial conversation, choosing 45–6
  school improvement, discussions in terms of 47
  solution-focused 46, 50
  stakeholder's priorities, understanding 45
  trust and rapport, building 45
  using non-defensive communication 51
process-driven accountability 151
professional accountability 150
professional confessions 60
professional development (PD) *see* Deputy

Headteacher professional
  development; support
  staff development; teacher
  development
professional perspective
  Andrew Percival 96–8
  Anna Woodcock 103–4
  Attiye Passey 135–6
  Clare Hoods-Truman 211–12
  Guy Shears 179–83
  Gwyn Ap Harri 14–17
  Hannah Abbiss 37–9
  Joanna Tompkins 225–6
  Josh Goodrich 163–6
  Richard Skilbeck 192–5
  Sally Alexander 6–7
  Sam Gibbs 75–7
  Stuart Milne 5
  Swabra Lloyd 199–200
psychological safety 138–42,
  157, 158, 160, 167
  vs. accountability for
    performance 148–9, 151
  principle-based framework
    146–7

relationships, establishing and
  managing 35, 215
  authentic leadership for
    40–4, 52–6
  power imbalances 44–55
  problem solving see problem
    solving strategies
  with stakeholders 43–4
reluctant leaders 177–8, 216
*The researchEd Guide to
  Curriculum* (Percival) 88
Rogers, Carl 138
Rosenshine, Barak 146

Schein, E.H. 28, 29
school culture 28–30
School Development Plan
  (SDP) 119–25
school leadership models,
  hierarchy of 13
self-reflection 31, 63–5
Senior Leadership Team (SLT)
  19, 60, 101, 119, 127, 145,
  152, 174, 178
shared accountability 152,
  153–4, 167
shared understanding 20, 24,
  25–8, 66, 73, 97, 111
Shears, Guy 179–83
Sherrington, Tom 40
Sims, S. 81, 156, 162
Skilbeck, Richard 44, 192–5
Skipp, A. 126
Smart, P. 26
stakeholders 43
  priorities and goals 45
standards
  consistency 58, 68, 69–70
  slipping of 57, 71
standards, setting 58–9
  evidence-informed
    framework 73–4
  expertise support in 74
  student needs 72–3
Strickland, Sam 105
Style theory 36
support staff 115
  morale 115–16
  teaching assistants 126–7
support staff development 117,
  134–5, 216
  communication through
    leadership 126–7

decision-making process, involvement in 118
professional learning, supporting 133–4
School Development Plan (SDP), involvement in 119–25
sharing and collaboration 132
support staff engagement in PD 128–9
understanding support staff perspectives 117–18
whole school priorities, contribution to 129–30, 133

teacher development 137–8, 167
accountability 147–54, 158
effective professional development programmes 156–60
instructional coaching 160–6
principle-based framework 146–7
psychological safety 138–47, 157, 158, 160
teacher job satisfaction 81, 125
Tompkins, Joanna 225–6
Trait theory 35–6
Trent, R.J. 36, 37

trust 3, 15–16, 18–19, 28, 82, 144, 189, 206, 215
mistrust 72
trust, building 23–4, 45, 58–9, 74, 215
delegation in 59, 64–7
self-reflection 63–5
vulnerability, modelling 60–2, 63–4

values 105–7
values-based leadership 67–9
Van de Brande, J. 137
Visible Learning (Hattie) 155
vulnerability 60–2, 63–4, 68–9, 72

Weindling, D. 150
whole school leadership 110–12
behaviour 99–110
curriculum 87–99
delegation *see* delegation
personal development 102–5
Why Should Anyone Be Led by You? (Goffee & Jones) 40
Willingham, Dan 88
Wolff, R. 67
Woodcock, Anna 102, 103–4, 105
Wright, N. 19

Zuccollo, J. 137